1/33

C0-DKM-324

POLICY STUDIES IN EMPLOYMENT AND WELFARE NUMBER 40

General Editor: Sar A. Levitan

Productivity:
Problems, Prospects, and Policies

Sar A. Levitan
Diane Werneke

The Johns Hopkins University Press
Baltimore and London

© 1984 by The Johns Hopkins University Press
All rights reserved
Printed in the United States of America

The Johns Hopkins University Press, Baltimore, Maryland 21218
The Johns Hopkins Press Ltd., London

Library of Congress Cataloging in Publication Data
Levitan, Sar A.
   Productivity—problems, prospects, and policies.

   (Policy studies in employment and welfare; no. 40)
   Includes bibliographical references and index.
   1. Industrial productivity—United States.
2. Gross national product—United States.   3. Production
(Economic theory).   4. United States—Economic policy
—1981–   .   I. Werneke, Diane.   II. Title.
III. Series.
HC110.I52L48   1984   338´.06´0973   83–22184
ISBN 0–8018–3022–2
ISBN 0–8018–3038–9 (pbk.)

HC
110
.I52
L48
1984

Contents

257287

CONTENTS

Preface

The American economy is still the most productive in the world. We currently produce about one-third more per worker than the Japanese, and at least 10 percent more than West Germany, our closest competitor in Europe.

Yet this preeminent industrial position is not unassailable. Americans have become increasingly preoccupied with diminished productivity growth. Most other industrial nations have improved their productivity over the past two decades at a much faster pace than the United States, and several countries have surpassed American productivity in highly visible and important industries, notably steel and automobiles.

Relative to other nations, there can be no doubt that our lead is dwindling. Between 1960 and 1982, Japanese productivity grew more than three times as fast as U.S. productivity, and even Britain's faltering economy could boast an average gain that was 33 percent above the U.S. rate. Today, as the economy moves out of the worst recession in the post–World War II period, the United States is experiencing a resurgence of productivity. It remains to be seen whether we can sustain a growth rate comparable to the rates of our major competitors over the long term.

Does it matter? No one who understands the critical role that productivity plays in our national economic and social well-being argues that it does not. In the past century, rising productivity has virtually defined the United States as a nation, both to itself and to others. Today American workers produce on the average about four times as much in an hour as the worker of fifty years ago. As a result, they work less hours, are healthier and safer, and have far more material possessions than their grandparents or parents. Our prosperity, our ability to compete internationally, our opportunities to accomplish more than our parents, and most critically our capacity and willingness to share our wealth, domestically and internationally, depend on sustained productivity growth.

This productivity primer focuses on critical areas that seem to be causing our lagging productivity growth and on the preconditions for a successful strategy for boosting America's performance. Part I reviews the sources for productivity measurements and assesses their reliability. An examination of the major economic and institutional factors that have presumably accounted for the nation's lackluster productivity performance follows. Part II scrutinizes the proposals presented for the revival of productivity growth, a ground well trod by many analysts, but with a different focus. The conclusion reached here is that judicious investments in labor market programs, both private and public, could enhance productivity, but first consensus must be reached on developing effective macroeconomic measures.

A great deal of confusion persists about the productivity concept. The term is subject to diverse interpretations because it means different things to different people. Even when it is carefully defined, the data to measure productivity may be inadequate.

The gaps regarding the measurement of productivity are matched by disagreement over the causes and cures of the nation's poor productivity performance. Analysts have generally viewed the issue from two perspectives. Economists have tended to focus on the impacts of macroeconomic variables, such as the slow rate of capital investment, declining and expanding economic sectors, the changing composition of the labor force, or the economy's shift from goods-producing to service industries. After identifying the importance of capital formation and technology, they have often overlooked institutional factors that directly influence the investment climate and the cultural impact of destabilizing inflationary biases that are built into the economy.

Labor market or industrial-organization analysts, on the other hand, have viewed productivity more in terms of the interactions between managers and their employees. They blame the prevailing adversarial relationship between management and labor, as well as the failure of many business leaders to properly manage their organizations and motivate their employees, for the slowdown in America's productivity growth. On the assumption that the practices and techniques of other nations can be transplanted to the much more contentious and individualistic American environment, they have argued that the adoption of industrial-organization models prevalent in Japan and Europe would lead to improved productivity growth in the United States.

Both approaches have helped to illuminate the multifaceted nature of the problem, but neither has provided a clear prescription for curing the maladies. While the Reagan administration has revised the tax code to encourage savings and investment, it has undermined the potential productivity gains from those changes by running huge budget deficits. This has forced the government to borrow an ever-larger proportion of the nation's savings, which in turn has resulted in high interest rates that have actually dampened investment and savings. The Reagan administration, which has insisted that government intervention has been a key contributor to lagging productivity, has not only increased the size of the federal government but has also shifted government resources from the most-productive activities (such as research and development, infrastructure investment, and education and training) to the least-productive ones (defense).

In contrast to the Reagan supply-side experiment, other observers have advocated a national industrial policy that favors an activist government role in prompting growth industries and in helping older ones to become more competitive. Whatever success this approach may have in Japan and other countries, it may be difficult or impossible to apply it to the United States. For an industrial policy to work, it must be backed by a national consensus of government, business, labor, and the public. There are no signs that such an agreement is attainable in the United States.

Within the company, participatory management and improvements in the quality of work life have been extolled by many analysts. The evidence, however, seems to be far from conclusive that the experiments, based largely on foreign experience, can be adopted for American industry. The experience of other nations cannot be easily transferred, because it fails to take into account the complexities of industrial relations and the adversarial positions traditionally taken by American labor and management. Company policies that link employee rewards with the success of the enterprise appear to be a more promising approach.

The government can help employers and workers adjust to the changes necessary for improved productivity growth. For example, programs that help promote greater job security and mobility of labor and capital could make workers and entrepreneurs more willing to accept the challenges of technological change. Improvements in education and training could cushion the problems associated with dislocations caused by the introduction of new technologies or imports. Investments in regional and local economic development and infrastructure rebuilding could encourage entrepreneurial efficiency while helping to preserve the social capital of many communities. If the government is to promote maximum productivity growth, it must be willing to help those whom growth and change leave behind. Otherwise, the individuals, firms, or communities that are threatened will seek to halt the changes from which productivity grows.

Sar A. Levitan
Diane Werneke

Acknowledgments

The authors are indebted to Jerome Mark of the Bureau of Labor Statistics, Richard Belous and Charles Stewart of the George Washington University, and Edgar Weinberg for their helpful critical comments, to Bobby Webster for preparing the manuscript for publication, and to Penny Moudrianakis of the Johns Hopkins University Press for editorial improvements.

This book was prepared under an ongoing grant from the Ford Foundation to the Center for Social Policy Studies of the George Washington University. In accordance with the foundation's practice, complete responsibility for preparation of the volume was left to the authors.

PART I

The State of Productivity

1

Productivity: Concepts and Trends

Productivity trends now share the limelight with fluctuations in unemployment, prices, and gross national product as major indicators of the nation's economic health. The declining rate of productivity growth in recent years has been identified as a key factor behind the difficulties besetting the American economy. An increase in the productivity growth rate is assumed to be a necessary condition for sustained economic recovery. Because productivity is critical to the nation's international competitiveness, rate of inflation, and standard of living, it has been a major concern not only of analysts but also of public and private policymakers. The concept remains poorly understood, however, and productivity per se is difficult to measure. It is not a relatively straightforward count like the number of unemployed people or the magnitude of the gross national product.

Different Perceptions

Productivity means different things to different people. To assembly-line workers, productivity may be associated with work effort—the number of bolts per hour they must tighten. To a plant manager, productivity may be a measurement of output—the number of widgets per day the plant can produce. The executive may focus on the profitability of the plant, while the consumer may be concerned with the quality of the products and their prices. All these different views associate productivity with the level of output (or reward) obtained for a given level of input (or effort). However, workers, managers, and consumers often have different notions as to what the real outputs and inputs of an assembly line, plant, or shopping expedition are. For analysts of economic performance, productivity denotes the *efficiency* with which resources—people, tools, knowledge, and energy—are used to produce goods and services for the marketplace.

Productivity, then, does not necessarily measure the effort workers put into their tasks. One worker may have better tools than another and consequently may produce more with less effort. As one analyst has noted, if productivity were defined in terms of effort exerted, the building of the pyramids in ancient Egypt would mark a peak period of productivity growth.[1] Economic analysts are therefore concerned with measuring not only human effort but the other factors that go into the production process as well.

The economic analyst's concept of productivity also differs from the plant manager's view of work measurement because the latter tells us nothing about each task's contribution to final output. For the analyst, productivity is concerned with the relationship between inputs and the final product. It is also distinct from the idea of profitability, which reflects financial as well as efficiency factors. While most productive companies are profitable, not all profitable companies are productive. Some may benefit from market power or from fortuitous circumstances.

An efficiency concept of productivity, however, is narrower than the idea of product quality, for economic efficiency is concerned only with the output of goods and services and not with how well the products meet consumers' needs or wants. Productivity data, for example, focus on the number of autos produced with the resources available, not on how long they last or how many gallons of gasoline it takes to keep them on the road. Productivity, then, is a concept of

4

production rather than a measurement of consumption or social welfare. Productivity indicators may be associated with a level of material well-being, but they reveal little about the distribution of income or about the social and political implications of changes in the nation's standard of living.

The measurement of productivity focuses entirely on market activity. Most aggregate productivity indexes are derived from the national income and product accounts which measure economic transactions in terms of purchases of goods and services and payments to the factors of production (i.e., labor, capital, or natural resources). The concept and measurement of productivity is consequently closely linked to market activities. With the development of social indicators that measure other dimensions of well-being, and with nonmarket activities such as safer products or cleaner air, economic information is only gradually beginning to move beyond market transactions.

As a concept of efficiency, productivity falls short as an indicator of how well the economy as a whole is using its resources. Because productivity measurements are concerned exclusively with the resources used in the production process, the concept ignores the wastes that unemployment entails. One economist has suggested that a more meaningful concept of productivity would take into account the hours that workers are available for work; such a concept would measure labor time lost due to forced idleness.[2]

A broad definition of productivity measures the relationship between the quantity of goods and services produced during a period of time and the input of labor, capital, and natural resources used in the production process. The relationship between output and inputs is highly dynamic. Over time the technology used in production will tend to change, and this can vastly alter an economy's productivity levels. Improvements in the education and skills of the labor force, changes in the degree of utilization of plants and equipment, and shifts in the skill and quality of an organization also will alter the relationship between output and inputs. An improvement in any of these factors will result in improved productivity.

Productivity growth rates have a major influence on the flow of resources, the economic development of a nation, and employment and investment opportunities. As first recognized by Adam Smith two centuries ago, productivity is the almost miraculous force that enables the wealth of a nation to vastly increase as the hours of work, or effort, are reduced.

The importance of estimating productivity changes accentuates the conceptual and definitional problems associated with their measurement. In the goods-producing sector—say, in manufacturing, where output is readily identified—performance can be estimated with a reasonable degree of confidence. But even in this sector, industries experiencing rapid technological change present measurement problems. However, in the service-producing sector—and in construction, where units of output are more difficult to define or to measure—the meaning of the statistics is far more ambiguous. As discussed in the appendix to this chapter, there is a great deal of uncertainty among analysts as to the reliability of data for these sectors.

The measurement problems become more difficult in the analysis of productivity trends. The tremendous shifts in employment from the goods-producing sectors into services, the changes in paid-for leisure patterns, which have affected the measurement of labor input, and the rapidly changing technology of sectors like the computer industry may have resulted in underestimated productivity growth. The increased public demand for social goods such as clean air and safer workplaces—which are not included in measured output—has exacerbated the difficulties of comparing productivity rates over time. Not surprisingly, there is little agreement among analysts as to the extent of the downward bias.

The weaknesses in the statistics also affect international comparisons, although to a lesser extent. The problems here may be less serious because the Bureau of Labor Statistics (BLS) adjusts data from other countries to U.S. definitions and focuses its attention on the manufacturing sector, where U.S. productivity information is most reliable. Manufacturing, however, accounts for only about a fifth of total U.S. employment, and consequently comparisons based exclusively on these industries may be misleading. Clearly, published estimates of U.S. productivity trends as well as international comparisons should be stamped with caveat emptor warnings.

Productivity Trends

Despite the difficulties in measuring productivity and the probable downward biases, mentioned above, the evidence is overwhelming that U.S. productivity growth has been declining in recent years compared with trends during the two decades following World War II. U.S. productivity growth has also lagged relative to the rates achieved by most other major industrial countries. The increase in labor productivity (i.e., output per work hour) in the business sector—the most frequently used measure—slipped from an average annual growth rate of 3.2 percent between 1948 and 1965 to 2.3 percent from 1965 to 1973 to below 1 percent in the following decade. The new BLS multifactor productivity measure, which relates output to both labor and capital, showed a similar pattern of deceleration, dropping from a 2.0 percent annual growth rate between 1948 and 1973 to a 0.1 percent rate thereafter (Table 1). U.S. productivity growth rates have lagged behind those of Western Europe and Japan throughout the postwar period, with the result that the products of some American industries have come under increasing competitive pressures at home and abroad. This, in turn, has had adverse consequences for the employment and income of many U.S. workers.

The post-1973 decline in productivity growth was pervasive throughout the nonfarm economy. The slowdown in manufacturing was particularly widespread in the steel and copper industries and in transportation equipment. Productivity growth also slowed in mining, construction, utilities, services, and trade.

In several mining sectors, productivity has actually declined during the past decade. The depletion of oil resources has meant that it takes more hours of work to produce a barrel of oil. Other mining activities have also been affected by depletion, particularly underground coal mining. Moreover, health and safety and environmental-protection

Table 1. U.S. productivity growth has declined sharply during the past decade

Labor productivity	Average annual percentage changes			
	1948–1955	1955–1965	1965–1973	1973–1982
Business sector	3.3	3.1	2.3	0.7
Nonfarm	2.6	2.6	2.0	0.5
Manufacturing	3.1	2.9	2.8	1.0
Durable	3.0	2.4	2.4	1.0
Nondurable	3.1	3.8	3.7	1.3
Multifactor productivity				
Business sector	2.5	2.3	1.4	0.1[a]
Nonfarm	2.1	2.0	1.2	0.0[a]
Manufacturing	2.5	2.6	2.1	0.4[a]

SOURCE: Bureau of Labor Statistics.
[a]1973–1981.

regulations have had an impact on measured productivity. For example, the filling in of open-pit mines and the provision of better ventilation and more tunnel supports in underground mines required added hours of work to produce a ton of copper or coal.

In utilities, much of the explanation for the drop in productivity growth rests with the rise in energy prices and with subsequent consumer efforts to conserve energy. Electric and gas companies employ most of their workers in maintaining distribution networks and in monitoring and maintaining facilities. These workers are needed no matter how much gas or electricity is produced. Consequently, when demand and output are rising, productivity increases, but when output falls or grows at slower than anticipated rates, productivity declines. Conscious decisions to save energy by lowering thermostat settings and improving insulation have decreased the demand for gas and heating oil. Demand has also been reduced as electrical equipment, from computers to home appliances, has gradually become more energy efficient. As in many mining industries, the measured productivity of the utilities sector may have been adversely affected by the introduction of environmental regulations. Some utilities were very slow to recognize the implications of the decline in the growth of demand. The consequent financial problems will place real constraints on boosting productivity in this sector of the economy.

The apparent deteriorating performance in the construction and service sectors is more difficult to explain. Some analysts have claimed that the decline in construction has been illusory—a statistical artifact rather than a real trend because output is difficult to measure. Others trace the slowdown in construction productivity to the completion of the interstate highway system, suggesting it was much easier to build roads across Kansas than to repair them in New York City. The sparse data available on the service sector, combined with the difficulties of measuring output there, justify skepticism about the reliability of the reported declines in service-sector productivity. For example, measured productivity in commercial banking was lower in 1980 than in 1973. This is hardly creditable, however, given the amount of labor-saving technology that has been introduced during the period. On a broader scale, it would be proper to question the reported poor productivity performance of consumer and business services when one considers the growing use of computers in the processing of information, the core activity of many of these industries.

While the apparent slowdown in productivity growth has been pervasive, developments in manufacturing have been the subject of greatest concern. This is because manufacturing industries are responsible for the weakening of American competitiveness in key industries in international markets (Table 2). Not only Japan, France, and West Germany have experienced much faster rates of productivity growth than America, but the United Kingdom, Italy, the Soviet Union, and some developing countries also have experienced larger gains than the United States. Moreover, this loss of competitiveness has occurred at a time when international trade has become more important in our economy. Until recently, U.S. production depended mostly on the nation's vast and rich domestic markets. Since 1970, however, the percentage of GNP devoted to trade has nearly doubled. Between 1977 and 1980, the Commerce Department has estimated that 80 percent of new manufacturing jobs were created in export-related industries.

Even allowing for a generous margin of error in the statistics, it is

Table 2. For more than two decades U.S. manufacturing productivity growth has trailed that of other industrialized countries

Country	Average annual percentage changes		
	1960–1981	1960–1973	1973–1981
United States	*2.7*	*3.0*	*1.7*
Canada	3.6	4.5	1.4
Japan	9.2	10.7	6.8
France	5.5	6.0	4.6
West Germany	5.2	5.5	4.5
United Kingdom	3.6	4.3	2.2
Italy	5.8	6.9	3.7
Sweden	5.0	6.7	2.2
Netherlands	7.1	7.6	5.1

SOURCE: Bureau of Labor Statistics.

clear that productivity has been growing much more quickly in many other countries than in the United States. Although the level of U.S. manufacturing output per employee hour is still the highest of the major industrialized countries—and the growth rates of West European countries and Japan have started from a smaller base—the gap has narrowed significantly. All countries showed a sharp slowdown after the oil crisis in 1973, but even then the productivity growth of some of our major competitors was substantially higher than the rates experienced in the United States in the more robust postwar years.

The differences in international productivity rates have had a direct impact on trading patterns. From the end of World War II through the 1960s, the United States was the world's leading exporter of manufactured goods. By 1970 West Germany had surpassed the United States in exports, and a decade later exceeded it by 22 percent. In 1970 Japan's manufactured exports were 62 percent of the U.S. level, but by the end of the decade they had reached 85 percent of U.S. levels.

BLS disaggregated studies of manufacturing industries in four countries confirm this picture of disappointing U.S. performance.[3] Japan had the highest productivity gains in each of the manufacturing industries observed, followed, with very few exceptions, by West Germany and the United Kingdom. The United States was in last place. The BLS has also studied the recent performance of the iron and steel industry in Japan, West Germany, France, and the United Kingdom. It focused on this industry not only because it ranks high among basic manufacturing industries and because of public interest but also because comparable information was available. These data show substantial gains in productivity for the Japanese, French, and West Germans relative to the Americans. In 1964 Japanese output per hour in steel was 41 percent of the U.S. level; by 1980 it was 128 percent of U.S. output. For France, the comparable data were 47 percent of U.S. levels in 1964, 86 percent in 1980. West German productivity was only half that of the United States in the early 1960s, but by 1980 it had surpassed U.S. productivity. Only the United Kingdom showed no relative gain.

Recently the United States has experienced a resurgence in productivity growth as the economy has pulled out of a severe recession. Whether the robust 4 percent rise in productivity during the first half of 1983 can be sustained remains an unanswered question. West European countries and Japan are also likely to experience substantial increases in productivity as they emerge from the world-wide economic slump. Productivity performance remains a central concern in the United States and in other nations, for economic and social issues will be affected by productivity trends.

Economic and Institutional Factors

The picture that emerges at present is one of lagging economic performance and productivity growth. Why has this slowdown occurred? Why should a nation that was the world's leading engine of growth for more than a generation suddenly find itself falling behind? Have Americans, since 1973, become too complacent about expanding the economic pie? Or are we simply experiencing an inevitable adjustment process as the fruits of technological advances spread more evenly around the world?

These questions have been vigorously debated in recent years, and a number of competing hypotheses have been advanced. Because the

11

problem is pervasive and complex, each of the major competing theories deserves scrutiny. While by no means mutually exclusive, these reasons can be broadly classified as economic and institutional.

The economic approach to assessing productivity performance tends to emphasize the macroeconomic factors that contribute directly to growth: inflation and cyclical changes in demand, investments in new plants and equipment, the development of new technologies, and the skills and experience of the labor force. In contrast, the institutional approach concentrates on the role of behavior, attitudes, and interactions among the major economic participants. Drawing from the experience of countries and firms with successful productivity records, some analysts have argued that the key to explaining the poorer performance of the U.S. economy lies in the structure of labor-management relations and in the organization of the workplace. While each school of thought has provided valuable insights into the current productivity problem, each has left critical gaps in understanding the problem and hence in developing adequate solutions.

Appendix: The Measurement of Productivity

This appendix examines in more detail the concepts and methods that go into forming productivity estimates. Econometric research in the area has recently involved new concepts and data aimed at solving old problems in this field.

The most common indicator used to measure productivity is expressed as the ratio of output to the number of employees or to employee hours. This ratio does not indicate the specific contribution of labor alone, although it is often interpreted in this way. For example, the number of acres a farmer can plow per day is obviously a function of the size of his tractor and plows, even though the ratio appears to be a measure of the productivity of his labor.

The labor ratio is the most pervasive indicator of productivity because labor is almost universally required to produce goods and services—for the time being, no robots produce their offspring without human help. Aside from the fact that labor input is easier to measure than other factors of production, almost every type of capital, energy, or raw-material input reflects the cumulative cost of the labor used to produce it.

Several sources of labor productivity data are available.[4] The basic data are derived from the national income accounts and the Bureau of Labor Statistics' current employment statistics program and the Current Population Survey. Using these data, the BLS reports quarterly the output per hour of all persons in the private business economy, the nonfarm business sector, and in manufacturing. The BLS also estimates the output per employee in domestic nonfinancial corporations. In addition, annual indexes are reported for each major industry in manufacturing, mining, transportation, communication, public utilities, services, and trade. (Because of insufficient industry coverage, the BLS does not provide aggregate estimates for non-manufacturing sectors.) These indexes reflect the level of productivity at any given point in time relative to the level of productivity in the base period. For example, in 1982 the productivity index was 101 compared to its 1977 base of 100.

The measurement of labor productivity reflects changes in efficiency over time, but it reveals little about the reasons accounting for these changes or their sources. Labor productivity may be growing because capital is being substituted for labor, the result being more efficient output, or, alternatively, because more highly trained workers are being employed. Consequently, analysts have developed multifactor measurements to elucidate the components contributing to changing productivity. These indicators relate output to more than one factor of production—for example, output per unit of labor and capital combined. Because the resulting productivity estimates offer a more complete accounting of the factors used in production, they fluctuate less widely than labor productivity statistics.

Multifactor productivity estimates are generally derived from models that attempt to delineate the sources of economic growth. In the absence of a consensus about treating difficult conceptual and data problems, there are almost as many estimates of multifactor productivity as there are analysts dealing with the subject. The estimates

13

Table 3. Denison's sources of economic growth, 1948–1973

Contributing factors	Annual growth rate (%)	Percentage of growth rate
National income	3.65	100.0
Factor inputs	2.13	58.3
Labor	1.42	38.9
Capital	.71	19.4
Land	0.00	0.0
Output per unit of input	1.52	41.6
Advances in knowledge[a]	1.10	30.1
Improved resource allocation	.29	7.9
Legal and human environment (regulations and crime)	−0.04	−1.1
Dwelling occupancy ratio	−0.01	−0.3
Economies of scale	0.32	8.8
Irregular factors (weather, strikes, intensity of demand)	−0.14	−3.8

SOURCE: Edward F. Denison, *Accounting for Slower Growth* (Washington, D.C.: Brookings Institution, 1979), p. 104, table 8-1.

[a]Primarily reflecting advances in technological knowledge as applied to the organization, processes, and tools of production.

by Edward Denison have received prominent recognition (Table 3). In 1983, the Bureau of Labor Statistics began publishing annual multifactor productivity estimates. The initial publication presented these data back to 1948. Time will tell whether the new BLS estimates will become the "official" data on the subject.

Measurement Problems

The adequacy and usefulness of productivity indicators is limited by the availability of data. Consider the difficulty of measuring output in government or nonprofit institutions, whose products are not exchanged in the marketplace. The output of service industries also is difficult to quantify—is the productivity of a teacher with forty students in the classroom double that of an instructor with twenty students? In addition, problems abound in measuring output in industries affected by rapidly changing technology or steadily improving products. Moreover, the quantification of resource inputs is not necessarily straightforward.

Output.   Difficulties with productivity indicators of output arise especially in industries with no clearly quantifiable product. The most obvious case is the government, where there can be no measure of final output because so many of the government's activities, such as education or national defense, are not explicitly bought and sold in the marketplace. In the absence of market valuation, analysts have traditionally estimated output change in terms of movements in employment. Since output by definition is equal to input, measured productivity—the ratio between the two—must remain constant. Because the inclusion of such a productivity measure would significantly bias estimates for the economy, the government sector, which accounted in 1983 for nearly 16 percent of all civilian employment, is excluded from the nation's officially published productivity statistics. This is a significant omission not only because of the size of the sector but also because of the increases in productivity that have taken place in many government operations.[5]

Measurement of the output of nonprofit institutions presents a similar problem, since most nonprofit services are not bought and sold in the marketplace. These activities also are excluded from official productivity measures. The scope of nonprofit services— college education, health care, and various philanthropic activities— has grown rapidly in recent years. Together, the nonprofit sector and government account for more than one-third of the expenditures cited in the gross national product and nearly a third of the nation's total employment.

Determining the output of many other service-producing industries is also problematic because determining a quantifiable "unit of service" is necessarily arbitrary and sometimes next to impossible. The Bureau of Labor Statistics therefore provides estimates for only seventeen industries in this sector, covering less than 40 percent of service-sector employment. Service-producing industries as a whole account for three-quarters of total U.S. employment. While industries such as transportation and public utilities are included in the productivity count, there are significant gaps in the data on finance, real estate, insurance, and wholesale trade. These omissions are par-

15

ticularly troublesome because many of these industries are experiencing rapid change—and potentially an increase in productivity—as computer technology is applied in their operations.

Even where productivity estimates are made, they are sometimes biased downward because output data are partly derived from input data, which tend to hold the productivity ratio constant. Outside the public and nonprofit sectors, which are excluded from the productivity count, this problem is most notable in the construction industry. Because the value of an output such as a building reflects extraneous factors dependent upon the structure's location and the purpose for which it is to be used, the ratio of building cost to selling price does not necessarily reflect the efficiency with which the building was erected. Because two identical buildings may have different prices, output is estimated by the cost of labor and materials, which means that the output data are dependent on inputs. In effect, the productivity indexes for the industry tend to be little more than cost indexes. Another industry where labor input is used in part to derive output is banking. Yet banking services are being revolutionized, and productivity is increasing rapidly because of the introduction of new electronic equipment.

Quality Change. Perhaps the most difficult problem in the construction of productivity estimates is how to incorporate changes in quality into output data.[6] Even within the same industry, outputs are not identical, and consequently they must be estimated by dollar value rather than by physical volume and then adjusted for price change in order to arrive at "real" output. Where a product or production technology is improving rapidly this technique may fail to capture the real improvement in productivity.

At present, the price indexes that are used for adjustment purposes take into account improvements in a product which are associated with a higher cost of production. For example, if automobile manufacturers introduce a radio as a standard feature on new models, the extra cost of producing the radio is subtracted from the retail price and thus is treated as a quality change rather than a price change.

Consequently, when consumers pay more for models with radios, real output rises, The extent to which productivity rises depends on the number of extra inputs used to produce the new radios.

However, other quality changes are not associated with an increase in the cost of production and are not accounted for in price deflation. New cars may offer greater fuel efficiency than the models they replace, and new computers introduced over the past twenty years have offered ever-greater memory and computing power at ever-lower prices. Clearly, the new models are more productive than the old ones, but the improved quality is not reflected in the productivity measurements. Assuming that the factor inputs required to produce the new computers are no greater than those needed to make the old models (and, in fact, are probably much less), productivity is substantially underestimated.

The difficulties of accounting for quality change associated with technological improvements are no less apparent when new products are introduced. When electronic calculators were first marketed, their cost was a fraction of the cost of the rotary calculators they replaced. However, rather than allow them to reflect the vast decline in price, manufacturers of the electronic devices treated them as a new product and linked them into the price index without a price change.

Many other innovations provide new services or allow old services to be produced at lower cost. Jet engines have improved the quality of airline service, and consumer appliances have been improved over the years in terms of energy efficiency and reduced repair requirements. The fact that these quality improvements have not been accounted for in price indexes means that price increases have been overstated while real output and productivity have been underestimated. This problem is likely to increase as new electronics technology is introduced in a wide range of goods and services.

The difficulties in measuring output accurately—both those associated with government and nonprofit industries and those associated with quality improvements—tend to bias measured productivity downward. Over time it appears that these factors have resulted in a significant cumulative underestimation of the nation's productivity.

Input. The measurement of inputs is also beset with conceptual as well as data problems. Even the labor productivity index, the most widely used estimate, is not immune to these difficulties. As currently reported by BLS, this index measures output per paid worker hour rather than hours worked. The difference between the two is accounted for by paid vacation and paid sick leave, work breaks, and machine downtime. Because employees are not producing goods or services when they are away, hours worked rather than hours paid for is the appropriate concept for measuring productivity.

Since the number of hours worked in recent years has represented a declining proportion of hours paid for, the published data tend to understate productivity growth. BLS data indicate that the change in any one year has been small. But cumulated over a longer time, it could have produced a significant downward bias in growth estimates. In addition, the University of Michigan's Survey Research Center data indicate that hours actually worked as a proportion of time spend at the workplace also have decreased. This further compounds the downward bias of the productivity statistics.[7]

Another difficulty with the BLS establishment data is that they do not include an estimate of the hours of all employees. The hours worked by supervisory, professional, and technical employees are estimated from other sources, and the hours worked by proprietors, unpaid family employees, and farm laborers are derived from data gathered in the bureau's Current Population Survey. Also, the sample of small firms in the establishment survey, particularly in construction, trade, and services, is grossly inadequate. This difficulty has been compounded because bench-mark revisions, which are based on a universal count of all establishments, have not been made regularly in recent years. A presidential commission which investigated employment and unemployment statistics found an urgent need to upgrade the program for collecting hours data.[8]

Multifactor productivity analysts have tried to measure capital resources used in the production process. As noted, measuring the contribution of a unit of capital to the production of goods and services involves conceptual as well as technical problems. The BLS obtains a measurement of capital services from the stock of physical assets—equipment, structures, land, and inventories—and rental prices for each type of asset. The measurement of stock, in turn, is derived from accounts data and other sources on investment, as well as capital and service deterioration functions. The rental prices are derived from data on depreciation costs and estimates of rates of return on capital assets. Ideally, however, capital inputs should be treated as flows rather than as stocks to be depreciated. The flow of services provided by a machine would reflect the time that that particular equipment was in use and would be the logical counterpart of the hours worked by labor. But the flow of services from a machine is difficult to measure. In theory, economists have considered a rental rate for a machine to be in line with the wages paid for labor. But in reality most companies own the machine, and there is no real rental market to use as a guidepost for actual estimates. Depreciation, which in effect assumes that a machine loses efficiency with age, is only a proxy for capital flows. Moreover, the depreciation costs used in measuring productivity are based on formulas applied to equipment and buildings by accountants, and consequently may differ substantially from the actual output capacity of the structures and equipment.

Nonmarket Goods. Another difficulty in measuring productivity concerns a fundamental conceptual problem—how one should treat nonmarket inputs that contribute to cleaner air, safer workplaces, healthier employees. Expenditures of labor and capital made to produce these outcomes are included with other inputs, but analysts have traditionally not considered the benefits generated to be part of the output. If an electric power company installs new equipment to reduce toxic emissions, the amount of labor and capital used to generate a kilowatt hour of energy increases and productivity as conventionally measured falls. However, if cleaner air is valued, the measurement of output should include the benefits to the people who were previously adversely affected by toxic emissions, or, alternatively, the costs of the damage inflicted by the pollution should be subtracted from the value of the polluter's output.

What emerges is a difference between social and private productivity rates. Environmental, occupational health and safety, and related regulations oblige companies to boost capital or labor outlays to produce their goods or services, and such outlays lower their measured productivity. However, the productivity indexes of these companies ignore the societal benefits accruing to individuals from safer air, cleaner water, more abundant natural resources, and fewer injuries.[9]

The divergence between private, or conventionally measured, productivity and social productivity has increased substantially over the last decade with the growth of environmental and workplace regulations. This presents a problem for comparative productivity analysis with respect to gauging both domestic trends and international comparisons. The regulations in Japan, West Germany, and other countries are at least as stringent in some areas as those in the United States, but estimates of the relative costs of these standards are lacking. It may have been easier and less expensive to modify the relatively more modern West German and Japanese plants and equipment to meet clean air or occupational safety standards than was the case with the older, U.S. facilities.

Comparative Productivity

Unlike other economic indicators, such as unemployment totals, the absolute level of productivity has less meaning for the analyst than the comparative level of productivity. The conceptual and data-related problems in measuring outputs and inputs and in developing productivity indicators assume significance, therefore, if the error or the bias weakens the reliability of productivity comparisons over time or among different sectors of an economy or different countries.

Time Series. Not surprisingly, analysts do not agree whether measurement problems have been exacerbated in recent years, thereby obscuring or misrepresenting actual productivity trends in the United States. A National Academy of Sciences panel headed by Albert Rees found significant downward biases in productivity measurements. In concluded, however, that there was no evidence that errors had become more substantial in recent years.[10]

Other analysts have not been so confident, and they are concerned that biases may be growing. Citing the increasing number of workers in government (where output is not measured) and service industries (where output is difficult to measure), some analysts have argued that in recent years standard indicators have resulted in large underestimates of productivity growth.[11] Similarly, because of the way output is measured in the construction industry, the sharp decline in productivity in recent years may be more a statistical artifact than a sign of reduced efficiency. Even in the manufacturing sector, where measurement problems are least troublesome, the decline in measured productivity growth may be the result of failing to quantify the impact of quality change. The computer equipment industry is an obvious case in point.

The measurement of labor input also has been cited as creating an increasingly important downward bias in measured productivity. This would mean that labor input has been increasingly overestimated and productivity underestimated. Finally, the failure to include non-market goods in measurements of output has certainly complicated the analysis of productivity. Since society has elected to "purchase" many more of these goods in the past fifteen years, an increasing proportion of the national output has gone uncounted. Clearly these problems suggest that productivity growth may have deteriorated less than the statistics indicate.

International Comparisons. Measurement of comparative international productivity is even more complex than national productivity indexes. Statistical concepts and measurement methodologies vary widely among countries, for each nation has developed its statistics to meet domestic rather than international needs. In the absence of uniformity, the most commonly cited comparative indicator is gross

21

domestic product per employee. Although this broad indicator is based on internationally accepted national income accounting procedures, it is probably an inadequate measure of comparative efficiency. It tends to obscure the structural changes in an economy which have a direct influence on productivity performance. For example, all industrialized countries have undergone major shifts in employment from agriculture to nonagricultural industries—sectors with different levels of productivity. Gross domestic product also includes the government sector, which for statistical purposes the United States and most other countries assume to have zero productivity growth. Finally, productivity measures that are based on counting the number of employees ignore changes in the average number of hours worked. In countries where the number of hours worked annually has changed little in recent years—for example, Japan—productivity may be overstated.

For these reasons, international comparisons of productivity are more reliable for the manufacturing sector, where fewer measurement ambiguities exist. However, even within this sector's more narrow confines, practices differ in estimating productivity. The BLS has attempted to adjust the data from other countries to achieve greater consistency, but often not enough information is available to achieve uniformity. For example, different activities may be included in a certain sector by different countries. Auto repair work is labeled as "manufacturing production" in some countries, whereas in the United States it is regarded as a service activity. In other cases, the uniqueness of a country's industrial organization makes direct comparisons difficult. In Japan many activities in heavy industries, particularly steel and auto manufacturing, are subcontracted, a fact which may affect a particular industry's productivity relative to that of another country.

Other difficulties in comparing productivity trends in the manufacturing sector reflect differences in measuring output and labor inputs. Some countries use national income accounts to derive manufacturing output estimates while others use industrial production data. The differences between the series are often substantial. Labor input also accounts for measurement differences. Some countries exclude from coverage a number of the workers engaged in production. West Germany, for example, excludes from its productivity counts establishments that have fewer than ten employees. It is therefore difficult to estimate either the extent or the direction of bias.

International comparisons compound the problems of measuring productivity. However, as competition in international trade intensifies, economic intelligence becomes ever-more significant. Comparative productivity indexes provide insights, albeit limited, into the economic performance and the relative position of each competitor on the international scene.

2

The Productivity Problem: Macroeconomic Factors

Economists have explored a portfolio of reasons for the slowdown in productivity. Capital spending, regulations, energy prices, research-and-development expenditures, and changes in the demographic composition of employment all have been analyzed, separately or in combination, for their adverse effect on productivity.[1]

Analysts have not yet agreed what factor(s) led to the decline in the growth of U.S. productivity during the preceding decade. The wealth of competing explanations reflects their preoccupation with supply-side factors at the neglect of other equally critical variables—the behavior of inflation and unemployment. The latter may have influenced productivity trends to an even greater degree than purely supply factors. Monetary, fiscal, and international trade policies have been the key forces behind aggregate demand. Productivity growth depends upon aggregate demand as well as on supply.

Supply-Side Components

Over the years, economists have considered capital investment rates, spending for research and development, and labor force skills as the major contributors to economic growth.[2] More recently, they have expanded their models to account for the slowdown in America's productivity growth and its poor performance in comparison with other countries. The factors they have investigated include the extent of government regulation, the impact of higher energy prices, and the changing composition of output. Although none of the factors, individually or combined, can fully account for the dynamics of growth, each appears to play some part. The relative importance of each, however, remains a subject of debate among economists.

Capital Investment

If economists agree on any key factor in productivity analysis, it is the importance of capital investment, which affects productivity in two ways. First, the more capital labor has to work with (i.e., the higher the capital/labor ratio), the more productive labor becomes. A cook with two ovens can prepare more dinners per hour than a cook with only one. Second, the greater the rate of investment, the more likely it is that newer, more productive plant and equipment will be employed. A cook with a microwave can prepare more food than a cook with a conventional oven. Despite this general agreement on the importance of capital investment, there is considerable disagreement among analysts over the role of investment in the past decade's productivity performance.

A number of prominent economists, including past and present members of the Council of Economic Advisers, have argued that the capital/labor ratio is a major culprit responsible for the nation's poor productivity performance. While gross private investment in plants and equipment as a proportion of gross national product has changed little in recent years, the total number of hours of labor input has grown at faster rates. The net result is that capital/labor ratios have fallen. Depending on how capital investment is measured and on the sector of the economy under examination, somewhere between one-fifth and two-thirds of the slowdown in growth has been attributed by some economists to a fall in the capital/labor ratio.[3]

However, Edward Denison, a recognized authority on the subject, has found little evidence to support the decline-in-capital-intensity hypothesis and consequently believes capital formation has not been a

25

major contributory factor to the productivity slowdown.[4] Supporters of this view argue that BLS studies of multifactor productivity show that only about 14 percent of the slowdown in overall productivity growth observed between 1973 and 1981 could be attributed to a deceleration in the growth of capital per unit of labor input. In the manufacturing sector, the BLS found that the capital intensity of production had actually increased over that period.[5] However, in contrast, earlier BLS studies found that the rate of capital formation had played a significant role in the slowdown of productivity growth during the same period.[6]

While some confusion prevails in analyzing domestic trends, the importance of capital formation in fostering productivity growth seems somewhat clearer in comparative international studies (Table 4). During the twenty-five year period after World War II, Japan invested nearly one-third of its gross output in new plants and equipment. For West Germany and France the comparable proportion was about 25 percent. In contrast, the U.S. investment accounted for less than one-fifth of gross output. In parts of Western Europe and Japan, high investment rates represented a continuation of efforts to rebuild industries destroyed or badly damaged during the war. Nevertheless, capital investment has remained high in these countries

Table 4. Gross fixed investment in the United States has lagged behind that of most other industrialized countries

Country	Percentage of gross domestic product					Annual change in productivity, 1960–1980
	1960	1970	1974	1978	1980	
United States	17.9	17.6	18.4	19.3	18.2	2.7
Japan	29.5	35.5	34.8	30.8	31.7	9.4
West Germany	24.3	25.6	21.9	21.2	23.6	5.4
France	20.1	23.4	24.3	21.4	21.6	5.6
United Kingdom	16.4	18.6	20.3	18.1	17.8	3.6
Italy	22.8	21.4	22.4	18.7	20.0	5.9
Netherlands	24.1	25.8	21.8	21.3	21.0	7.3
Sweden	22.1	22.5	21.6	19.4	20.3	5.2

SOURCE: OECD, *Economic Outlook* (Paris: OECD, December 1981), p. 133; and U.S. Department of Labor, Bureau of Labor Statistics.

relative to that in the United States in more recent years. In 1980, Japan continued to invest nearly one-third of its output; West Germany, nearly a quarter; and France, Italy, and Sweden, about one-fifth. Only in the United States and the United Kingdom did investment account for less than 20 percent of national output, and they were at the bottom of the ladder with respect to productivity growth among industrialized countries.[7] The relatively greater rates of investment abroad have contributed to the faster growth in the capital intensity of production. Most comparative economic studies suggest that a significant proportion of variations in growth may be explained by this factor (Table 5).[8]

The identification of capital investment as a significant force behind poor U.S. productivity performance leaves the unanswered question, why does the United States invest relatively less than its competitors? The instability of aggregate demand during the last decade clearly played a key role. In addition, some economists have emphasized the growth of regulations and the impact of higher energy prices as factors which may have affected the U.S. economy more adversely than other countries.

Regulations

A number of observers have suggested that the imposition of new regulations has reduced measured productivity growth by allocating

Table 5. Gross fixed capital stock per hour worked was less in the United States than abroad

Country	Average annual compound rate of growth	
	1950–1977	1970–1977
United States	2.7	*1.8*
Canada	3.6	2.7
France	5.2	8.0
West Germany	5.9	7.1
Italy	4.9	7.3
Japan	6.8	8.4
United Kingdom	4.0	4.4

SOURCE: Angus Maddison, "Long Run Dynamics of Productivity Growth," *Banca Nazionale del Lavoro Quarterly Review,* March 1979, p. 19, table 5.

resources to fund unmeasured outputs such as a cleaner environment or a safer workplace. In addition, the application of new regulations is thought to be associated with considerable uncertainty, which tends to reduce innovation and investment. Some economists have estimated that imposition of regulations reduced the annual growth rate of productivity between 1973 and 1980 by 0.3 percent.[9]

While this analysis may help to account for some of the slowdown in domestic performance, it does little to explain our poor performance compared to that of our international trading partners. Not only did U.S. productivity lag behind that of many other countries prior to the introduction of regulations in the 1970s, but many of those whose performance has been superior since then have regulations that are at least as stringent as those in this country. For example, in 1980 the proportion of investment spent to meet environmental protection standards in West Germany accounted for nearly 6 percent of capital outlay compared with about 4.5 percent in the United States.[10] The Japanese have substantially expanded such expenditures in recent years as well.

On the other hand, the controversy and litigation that is built into U.S. regulatory processes may increase the level of uncertainty generated by new U.S. regulations, making them more disruptive than those of other nations. In Japan, government and business leaders typically reach a consensus regarding needed environmental or safety regulations (after considerable, often contentious, debate) and then proceed to implement them by law and private action. In the United States, the proposal of a new regulation typically marks the beginning of a process of lobbying and litigation that may last for decades. This discourages advance planning and efficient investment. The problem, then, is the American propensity to litigation, not regulation per se. Moreover, some analysts have argued that despite the uncertainty generated by new regulations, compliance with new standards may have brought unforeseen benefits to companies. New investments and technologies may have resulted in productivity boosts that would not otherwise have occurred.

Energy Prices

The steep rise in the price of oil following the 1973 embargo coincided with a slowdown in productivity growth in all industrialized countries. Consequently, the oil shock and the subsequent boosts in the price of energy have been viewed by many economists as key contributors to the poor performance of U.S. productivity.[11]

Higher energy prices contributed to inflation and resulted in aggregate-demand policies to counteract these moves. The net result was higher unemployment and a poorer investment climate, which in turn fed back on productivity and lowered its reported rate of growth.

The adverse effects of higher energy prices on productivity are caused by the substitution of less-productive alternatives—for example, labor for energy. In addition, plants and equipment designed when energy was cheap become uneconomical and obsolete faster when energy prices rise. Consequently, the amount of capital per worker declines unless the rise in energy prices also induces capital spending.

For these reasons post-1973 increases in energy prices may have reduced capital/labor ratios and, in turn, rates of productivity growth. Also, higher prices for products that use energy intensively—for example, man-made fibers and other petrochemical products—may have caused a shift in demand toward more labor-intensive, low-productivity goods, such as natural fibers and forest products. However, other analysts have argued that the value of energy in the production process is so small in proportion to total costs that its impact on productivity is insignificant.

Another possible effect of the oil price increase on U.S. productivity was its impact on corporate cash flows. Because the energy price increases were the economic equivalent of a large tax increase distributed to oil producers from oil consumers, their impact on capital distribution and employment may also have been disruptive. Beginning in 1973 huge amounts were siphoned off from the nation's businesses to the bank accounts of various oil-exporting nations and

29

to U.S. and foreign oil companies. To the extent that this capital was not recycled back to U.S. industry through U.S. banks, it had the effect of reducing the cash flow available to U.S. nonenergy business. There is uncertainty whether this effect was significant. Also, the United States may have been affected by the rise in energy prices more adversely than countries that used energy less intensively. The United States, which had the lowest-priced oil among the major industrial countries and the most energy-intensive economy, was forced to make more abrupt adjustments.

Research and Development

In addition to the factors that may have adversely affected capital investment, some analysts have also cited a slowdown in research-and-development expenditures.[12] These investments can be expected to boost productivity through the development of more efficient equipment and production processes. The National Science Foundation estimated that research-and-development expenditures in the United States as a proportion of GNP peaked at 3 percent in 1964 and then declined to 2.2 percent in 1977. Since then, investment in research and development as a proportion of GNP has continued to climb, rising to 2.65 percent in 1983.

It seems doubtful, however, that the decline in the 1970s affected productivity growth. Research and development funded by private industry accounted for about 1 percent of GNP between the early 1960s and mid 1970s. It has risen since then to an estimated 1.4 percent of GNP. Because of the relatively long time lag between investments in basic research, patenting, and commercialization of new products or processes, the reduction in aggregate R&D outlays could have had at most only a marginal impact on productivity performance. Consequently, it is unlikely that the slowdown in R&D expenditures has played a major role in domestic productivity performance.

Basic R&D expenditures do appear to correlate with productivity growth rates internationally, however. In comparison with other countries, West Germany and Japan show the highest proportion of output devoted to research and development exclusive of defense and space spending. The West German government provides subsidies for civilian industrial research, as does the Japanese government. In Japan, government assistance is given to government institutes for research work on electronics, electric cars, computers, aircraft engines, and steelmaking, and the research results are then disseminated to private industry. Given such planning and assistance, it is possible that research spending may be more cost-effective in Japan and West Germany than in the United States. The Economic Recovery Tax Act of 1981 provided special tax incentives for added spending in R&D through 1985.

Spending on research and development is, however, only one strategy for improving productivity by employing new technology. In many cases, it is more efficient for firms to buy technology directly, and over the postwar period many foreign companies have acquired their technology through patent licenses, technical agreements, and other methods. As these countries reach the technological frontier established by the United States, however, the quality and quantity of research-and-development spending should become an even more important component in productivity growth.

The Work Force

In addition to exploring the impact of capital formation, some analysts have emphasized the effect of changes in the age and sex ratios of the work force on productivity. Beginning in 1965, when the offspring of the postwar "baby boom" reached working age, many young and unskilled workers were added to the labor force. At the same time, an increased number of women joined the labor force, boosting further the proportion of relatively inexperienced workers. Presumably, these new workers have affected the rate of productivity growth adversely. In the United States, the Council of Economic Advisers has estimated that these demographic shifts reduced the nation's productivity growth rate by about 0.4 percentage point a year between 1965 and 1973, and by about 0.3 percentage point thereafter.[13]

If accurate, this analysis would help to explain the productivity differences between the United States and other countries. Most other countries also have experienced demographic shifts due to increased numbers of young people and rising female participation in the labor force. In Western Europe and Japan, however, the impact of the larger proportion of young people on the job market may have been cushioned to some extent by increased educational enrollment, which has postponed labor-force entry. In contrast, many young people in the United States combine work with their studies.

The evidence is far from conclusive, however, that the increased participation of women and young people in the labor force has reduced productivity. For one thing, these new entrants have higher levels of educational attainment than the average of the rest of the labor force. Presumably, a strong educational background is related to productivity because it is associated with the ability to understand and to adapt more quickly to change. Consequently, increased educational qualifications tend to facilitate technological advance and productivity growth. In fact, studies have shown that better-educated workers have an advantage in adapting to new technological developments relevant to their work.

A second difficulty with this argument is inherent in the way productivity is measured. Because wages are used in many industries as an approximation of the level of productivity, the lower rates paid to women may reflect pay discrimination rather than lower productivity. Also, women and younger workers tend to work part-time to a greater extent than the rest of the labor force, and part-time workers are generally less well paid than full-time workers.

Structural Changes

As economies grow and change, new and more productive industries arise while employment in older industries declines. The mechanization of agriculture presents an outstanding example of this.

Workers who had held low-productivity agricultural jobs found new and frequently higher-productivity jobs in manufacturing industries, thereby increasing the nation's total average productivity. On the other hand, the rapid increase in the number of workers in the service sector (where measured productivity growth is lower than in agriculture or manufacturing) has been cited as a possible explanation for reduced productivity growth in recent years.

In a recent study, Victor Fuchs, the foremost authority on service sector trends, found that the growth of services relative to industry accounted for only a small change in productivity trends over the post–World War II period.[14] The Council of Economic Advisers and the BLS also have found that the shift in employment to the service sector had little impact on aggregate productivity in the 1970s, because the growing sectors of the economy included both high- and low-productivity industries.[15] The service sector has experienced notable structural shifts as small, family-run enterprises have been replaced by large-scale and more efficient retailers. An OECD report on structural change in Western Europe, Japan, the United States, and Canada reached a similar conclusion: the explanation for the slowdown in total productivity growth has to be found within sectors rather than as a result of employment shifts among sectors.[16]

Other economists using different research methods, have found a notable and in some cases quite substantial impact on productivity due to the shift of employment to the service sector. Some have attributed as much as 40 percent of the decline in the nation's productivity to the growing employment in services.[17]

The decline in measured productivity in the service industries may be partially a result of improved services to consumers. During the 1970s many retail stores extended their shopping hours, in part to serve customers who were increasingly entering the work force. Because there was little or no increase in the volume of output sold but only an extension in the time when purchases were made, productivity by definition declined. However, anyone who has had to do the weekly food shopping on his or her lunch break would probably put the convenience in shopping ahead of measured productivity gains. In other countries the shift of employment to service activities may have had a less significant impact on observed productivity because the service sector is not yet as fully developed there as it is in the United States. Store hours have not been extended significantly in most West European countries, and Sunday shopping is a rarity.

Western Europe and Japan may have enjoyed productivity gains to a greater extent than the United States owing to other structural changes resulting from increased international trade. In Western Europe, the formation of the European Economic Community enabled member countries to specialize in the goods and services they produced most efficiently compared with other countries. They could also exploit economies of scale, thereby raising productivity. Similarly, Japan benefited from the trade liberalization brought about by international trade agreements. The increase in the size of their markets and the associated economies of scale were much greater for these countries than for the United States, where national companies already served very large markets.

Inflation and Unemployment

Fundamental but often-neglected factors affecting productivity growth are those connected with the business cycle. Fluctuations in demand as well as related swings in inflation are significant. Clearly, productivity growth is intimately related to aggregate demand forces, but we know little about the interaction between the state of the economy and productivity. Are the nation's economic problems a cause or an effect of the productivity slowdown?

Ample empirical evidence shows that in the short run the U.S. economy adjusts poorly to variations in demand. If demand falls in a business downswing, firms tend to cut output in an effort to adjust inventory stocks to sales. Plants produce fewer goods, and the utilization rates of plants and equipment fall. However, because of uncertainties about the extent and duration of the downswing, employers tend to delay adjusting the size of their work force, and output per worker falls. Similarly, in an upswing, employers are reluctant to begin hiring until they absorb the slack in capacity and assess the outlook. As a result of these lags over a business cycle, labor productivity tends to fall as output is reduced without a proportional reduction in labor input, and conversely it rises when demand recovers.

Over the longer run productivity plays a key role in determining growth in output by reducing production costs. As productivity rises during periods of renewed demand, it raises the real incomes of capital and labor. At some point in a recovery period employers become confident enough to add workers and eventually to add to their plant capacities through investments in new capital. The new investments presumably boost productivity, thereby increasing output, demand, and income further. It would appear, therefore, that sustained, balanced economic growth may make a substantial contribution to productivity growth by positively influencing investment spending, employment, and incomes. Conversely, prolonged recessions can have exactly the reverse effect as capital spending is deferred, productivity fails to improve, incomes decline, and the downward spiral repeats itself.

A Matter of Timing

The decline in measured U.S. productivity dates back to the 1960s and covers periods of both growth and recession. This may account in large part for the neglect of demand as a determinant of productivity trends. There is, however, further reason to question the long-term nature of the slowdown. If one examines productivity trends over business cycles one finds that except for a sharp deceleration in the 1953–1957 cycle, productivity growth ranged between 2.3 percent and 2.7 percent prior to 1973, when the growth rate slowed dramatically. Average annual nonfarm productivity growth rates from 1948 to 1981 (measured peak to peak) were as follows:

1948–1953	2.7
1953–1957	1.7
1957–1960	2.3

1960–1969	2.5
1969–1973	2.4
1973–1980	0.6
1980–1981	0.8

In this analysis, the alleged decline in growth in the late 1960s and early 1970s amounted to a slowdown of 0.1 percentage point, which may not even be statistically significant.

A Congressional Research Service study has explored the productivity fluctuations that occur during the three phases of business cycles: recession, when output falls; recovery, when production begins to turn upward; and expansion, when output surpasses its previous peak and then begins to turn down again in the next recession.[18] Viewing the business cycle in these three phases has the advantage of allowing one to separate productivity trends that resulted from cyclical fluctuations in demand from those which occurred during periods of expansion. In the latter case, productivity was not affected by lagged adjustments in employment or hours in response to changes in output. Consequently, an examination of growth during expansion phases alone provides an approximate view of secular trends in productivity growth. Based on this analysis, a Congressional Research Service analyst concluded that nonfarm productivity decelerated markedly after 1973 (Table 6).

The expansion phase 1960–1969 shows the strongest growth of any of the post–World War II phases. Yet it is during this period that some

Table 6. Nonfarm productivity has decelerated sharply since 1973

Business cycle	Average annual rates of productivity growth		
	Recession	Recovery	Expansion
1948–1953	0.6	11.6	2.0
1953–1957	0.5	5.4	1.2
1957–1960	2.2	6.0	1.1
1960–1969	1.0	8.3	2.5
1969–1973	1.1	8.4	2.4
1973–1980	−2.1	5.1	0.4
1980–1981	−0.6	4.1	−0.8

Source: Mary Jane Bolle, *Impact of the Business Cycle on Productivity Growth in the U.S. Economy* (Washington, D.C.: Congressional Research Service, 1982).

analysts believe a slowdown occurred. Indeed, the only other expansionary phase that approaches this growth rate is the expansion following the 1971 recovery of economic activity, after the deceleration in productivity was thought to have occurred.

What is also evident is the quite noticeable slowing of the trend after the 1973–1975 recession and the absolute decline associated with the 1980 recession. In fact, productivity trends were sharply lower in each phase of the latter two cycles than in any of the earlier postwar cycles. Thus it appears that 1973, not an earlier date, was the year our productivity woes began.

Demand Conditions

The significance of establishing 1973 as the beginning of the slowdown in U.S. productivity growth is that it points toward the role of macroeconomic performance in bringing about that deceleration. It not only suggests that many of the policy responses to economic conditions during the period have had a depressing impact upon productivity but it also raises questions as to whether existing institutional frameworks are adequate to meet the challenges of current economic problems.

The key feature of the post-1973 economy was accelerating inflation. Although inflationary pressures had been building for some time, stemming from excessive fiscal stimuli during the Vietnam era, they were brought to a head by the oil embargo in 1973 and by the quadrupling of oil prices that marked the embargo's end. At the same time, other commodity prices accelerated, producing a sharp rise in inflation. In response to these developments, economic policy turned from the management of high aggregate demand and low unemployment to combating inflation. Stringent monetary policy coupled with fiscal restraint sent interest rates soaring and demand plunging. Overall economic activity declined sharply, boosting unemployment to postwar highs. However, despite the sharp reduction in aggregate demand, the inflation rate never returned to its pre-1973 level, and it accelerated again in the late 1970s as food and oil prices again rose

37

sharply and cost pressures resulting from earlier inflation rates worked their way through the economy despite high unemployment and idle capacity. Renewed policy restraints starting in the late 1970s again boosted unemployment, interest rates, and idle capacity to record highs before inflation began to recede in 1982.

These developments affected productivity adversely in several ways. As suggested earlier, in the short run, cyclical variations in demand are directly associated with decelerations in productivity growth because of the lagged adjustment of labor inputs to decreases in output. Over a longer time period, inadequate and unstable demand dampens investment incentives because it increases the risks of undertaking new ventures. As decisions are postponed or canceled, spending falls and unemployment rises. This, in turn, adversely affects consumer spending, further depressing aggregate demand.

High and volatile interest and inflation rates exacerbated the economic difficulties as uncertainties about the costs of long-term investments and the future course of government policy to combat inflation further disoriented capital markets. Innovative investment and other high-risk economic activities, the sources of future productivity growth, were postponed. Instead there was a greater tendency to protect capital from inflation by speculating in nonproductive assets, such as collectibles, or to alter investment portfolios to hedge against inflation rates rather than maximize long-term gains. During the 1970s a noticeable concentration of funds was allocated to existing products rather than to the development of new products or processes.

Other nations were able to choose a better mix of macroeconomic policies to fight inflation without harming long-term productivity growth as much. The 1973 oil shock, inflation, and the subsequent recession brought about a sharp deceleration in growth in all the industrialized countries, but some nations weathered the storm better than others. As an indicator of the national macroeconomic performance of major industrialized countries, the New York Stock Exchange developed an "economic performance index" which charted movements in real output, consumer prices, and unemployment for the periods 1960–1973 and 1974–1980.[19] This index shows that the United States ranked sixth of the eight nations covered in both periods.

In Japan, although the inflation rate was quite high (averaging about 9.6 percent between 1973 and 1980 compared with 6.0 percent between 1960 and 1973), unemployment was kept at 2.0 percent of the labor force in the later period and even lower during earlier years. In West Germany, increases in prices were more moderate: only 4.7 percent on average in the post-1973 period compared with 3.2 percent earlier. Unemployment also was low, averaging about 3.3 percent, although West German definitions and means of measuring un-employment may tend to understate the figures somewhat.

Both of these countries managed to perform reasonably well despite their relatively greater dependence on oil imports as compared with the United States. The OECD attributed this to appropriate policy responses and economic adjustments. In West Germany, the severity of inflation was limited in part by wage restraints, which prevented a profit squeeze of the corporate sector. As a result, private fixed investment rose faster there than in most other OECD countries, and structural adjustment to the new energy situation was rapid. West Germany's productivity growth thus recovered after 1973. In turn, cutbacks in employment were cushioned by government support of work-sharing, job creation, and the export of "guest laborers" to other countries, thereby freeing jobs for the population at home.[20] Japan, according to the OECD, pursued a sustained countercyclical policy combined with an activist industrial policy throughout the period. In addition, wage restraints and the flexible deployment of labor were largely responsible for the country's relatively strong investment and productivity performance.[21]

Economic Stability and Productivity

At the macroeconomic level, inflation and productivity are closely intertwined. An inflationary environment is inimical to productivity growth because rising prices create uncertainties and tend to shift investment toward less-productive ventures, including speculation. However, fighting inflation by creating idle capacity in product and labor markets creates an equally unfavorable environment for productivity growth. Not only do companies experience a drop in efficiency associated with a downturn in economic activity but the resulting idle capacity depresses investment over a longer period of time. In contrast, a period of balanced economic growth provides the appropriate incentives to meet rising market demand by expanding capacity and inventory. The resulting income flows contribute to the continuing growth of aggregate demand.

Of course, some argue that aggregate demand has been higher in some periods of the post-1973 years than traditional measures would indicate. They argue that inflation accelerates at a higher unemployment rate than previously because of rigidities in the labor market and the changing composition of the labor force. Reflecting this hypothesis, the Council of Economic Advisers has revised downward potential GNP, which identifies the level of output above which unacceptable levels of inflation would occur.

However, the rationalization of creeping unemployment is not persuasive, considering the costs. The unemployment rate has dropped below 6 percent during only one year since the mid-1970s as compared with less than 5 percent during all but two years during the preceding similar period. The economy has not approached its optimal growth rate whatever measure of potential GNP is used.

These observations strongly suggest that the macroeconomic policies used to combat inflation have been inappropriate for fostering productivity growth. Fighting inflation with macroeconomic restraint has reduced price rises but at the cost of reduced output, employment, and productivity. However, the generation of additional aggregate demand, if not accompanied by wage and price restraints, would likely have contributed more to inflation than to economic expansion, again inhibiting productivity growth. It is therefore reasonable to conclude that a diagnosis of the productivity problem cannot ignore the institutional arrangements that deal with the core problem of wage and price determination. The productivity performance of other countries may have been stronger than that of the United States because of better macroeconomic management, resulting higher rates of investment, and more research-and-development spending. But these explanations beg the fundamental question of why these countries were able to adapt to changing economic circumstances more easily than the United States.

3

The Productivity Problem: Institutional Factors

Some leading analysts of productivity have realized that institutional and cultural forces—and not just macroeconomic factors—have had a significant impact on the U.S. economy both for good and for ill. Joseph Schumpeter, one of the outstanding economists of this century, noted that "the explanation of development must be sought outside the group of facts which are described by economic theory." It is "not possible to explain economic change by previous economic conditions alone," he asserted.[1]

Despite Schumpeter's insight, institutional and cultural factors often have been given short shrift. This is due in part to the difficulty associated with measuring these forces. By focusing on macroeconomic factors, analysts of productivity performance fail to illuminate the determinants of productivity at the plant or office level. To examine the latter involves viewing the organizational and social aspects of the enterprise. This approach offers frequently neglected insights into the productivity puzzle. This method of analysis also considers differences in norms and cultural patterns and how these relationships change over time.

In the past several years there has been increasing speculation that differences in decisionmaking patterns by business firms in different countries hold the key to variations in productivity performances among the major advanced industrial nations. In particular, the institutional arrangements in West Germany and Japan, the United States' competitors, have been cited as models to be emulated in order to achieve optimal productivity. Proponents of reforming the workplace have stressed the need for organizational change, including the provision of better labor-management communications, and the potential of raising productivity in the short run by changing employee attitudes.[2]

In the process of advocating adaptation of foreign experiences, analysts have extolled selected aspects of a particular system without featuring its drawbacks. Moreover, whatever the merits of the practices are in their native lands, they may prove unsuitable for the American environment. Systems of industrial relations are specific to each country, reflecting the customs, attitudes, and traditions of the society, and they are not easily transferrable across continents.

Participation and Productivity

Rejecting the prevailing U.S. economic doctrine, which tends to view the firm as a machine that maximizes short-run profits, students of organizational behavior regard an enterprise as a social system with gaps between actual and optimum performance. An organization may be resistant or unresponsive to management goals. Jobs may be incompatibly designed, given the existing skills of employees, or they may be inappropriately meshed. Information may be lacking, thereby forestalling smooth and coordinated work processes. The consequence is deficient control over the quality and quantity of production. Management can set its goals in broad terms, but at the lower levels there is considerable room for variation both in the interpretation of goals and in the effort made to meet them. In fact, one analyst suggests that, given incomplete information, employees tend to work in a way that is incompatible with the efficient utilization of resources.[3]

To achieve greater productivity, according to this view, management needs to share authority with workers by giving the employees a greater voice in determining production processes. Work reform and job redesign can improve the production process. New channels of communication can improve decisionmaking at all levels by spurring management efficiency and delegating responsibility to those actually performing the work.

Job satisfaction may also play a major role in worker productivity. One of the principal arguments advanced in favor of worker participation is that giving employees a greater share in decisionmaking can reduce alienation and, with it, nonproductive practices such as absenteeism, turnover, and poor-quality work. Workers are viewed as being less willing to accept authoritarian decisions just because they have stepped within the factory gate or office door.

Proponents of work reform argue that the spread of longer school attendance and the growth of the mass media have changed the qualifications, viewpoints, and aspirations of today's workers and have generated a demand for individual freedoms and rights on the job floor as well as in the political arena. Also, the rising living standards of the post–World War II era have extended workers' traditional concerns with satisfying basic needs to broader interests in working conditions, employment relations, responsibility, and recognition.

Advocates of work reform as a means to boost productivity have argued that American managers and workers would benefit by adopting foreign practices. The evidence that workers' participation schemes result in greater productivity is far from conclusive, however. Generalizing on the basis of case studies is unwarranted because it is difficult to identify the nature and extent of worker participation and because it is hard to isolate the impact of workers' participation from other organizational and technological changes affecting productivity.

The West German Experience

The West German and Japanese systems of worker participation have been touted as models for achieving organizational efficiency. In West Germany, participatory mechanisms have been established at two levels within the company: at the top and on the shop floor.[4] By law, workers have equal representation with shareholders on the supervisory boards of companies employing 2,000 or more workers. The supervisory board approves major decisions about investments, loans, and other activities affecting the company's balance sheet. In addition, the supervisory board selects a management board, which is responsible for day-to-day decisionmaking. Thus, in principle, West German workers' representatives share with owners the power to set policy. Also, through their right to select a labor director to sit on the management board, workers share in the day-to-day implementation of these policies. However, in practical terms, in the majority of companies workers' representatives play little more than an advisory role—they may be seen and heard but are not necessarily listened to. The chairman of the board is elected by the stockholders and retains control of the board and the real authority to run the company.

On the shop floor, workers' councils are elected by all employees. These councils have a voice in virtually all aspects of performance on the job, and they are, in consequence, much more powerful than American shop stewards or business agents. Although worker representation on company boards has received the most attention in the United States, workers' councils are the key element of the West German work force's participation in company operations.

A number of programs funded by the West German government have attempted to adjust working conditions by reorganizing jobs to expand worker discretion in, and responsibility for, daily work and quality control. In such cases, the organization of work has been reoriented around autonomous work groups, each of which is responsible for part of the production process; this arrangement gives every worker a voice in day-to-day decisionmaking.

Have worker participation efforts in West Germany improved that nation's productivity performance? The Biedenkopf Commission, established to review the system of codetermination, found that worker participation had served industry well and had not reduced the competitiveness of companies as some employers had feared.[5] The commission concluded that board representation had provided both employees and management with information that facilitated change within the company. Management found it useful to have a mechanism for informing employees of the company's situation and for encouraging cooperation. Employees believed that communication had been increased.

The chief contribution of worker participation to West German productivity seems to be that it has promoted industrial peace and acceptance of change. Workers' councils have provided a mechanism for handling grievances and disputes and have helped to prevent management decisions that could cause employee dissatisfaction. With respect to shop-floor experiments, however, little hard evidence is available on contributions to productivity.

The Japanese Experience

In Japan, worker participation is less institutionalized and instead is derived from the unique system of industrial relations that characterizes many large Japanese companies.[6] Lifetime employment is reinforced by a seniority-based system that establishes a steady progression of status and pay, a system that is based on the age of the employee rather than on the precise work done. The result is a flexible work force that is willing to perform a variety of tasks and to accept technological change. Finally, the fact that unions are organized on a company basis rather than by occupation or industry, as is the case in most other countries, tends to stimulate cooperation between the unions and management. It is in labor and management's mutual and lifelong interests for the company to perform well. The commonality of interests is underpinned by a bonus system whereby payments often amounting to two to four months' wages are paid to employees on the basis of the company's performance.

Because these features of labor-management relations are common in large companies, they tend to promote mutual interest and understanding. Decisionmaking in many Japanese companies is consensual in nature. Before any decision is made, consensus is sought at all levels of the company, a procedure known as *ringi*. Although time-consuming, the process stimulates an exchange of information and cohesion, and thus, once a decision is reached, it can be implemented with speed and support within the enterprise. This is reinforced in many companies by an extensive labor-management consultation system. Employee representatives have no formal veto power, but in practice many exercise considerable informal influence in company decisionmaking.

Shop-floor participation takes a more concrete form in Japan than in the United States. Adapted from the ideas of an American scientist, William Deming, quality control circles have proliferated in Japan. Currently these circles involve in one way or another more than one worker in every eight. Part of the reason they have caught on is that as a concept, quality control corresponds well to the attitudes fostered by the system of industrial relations: cooperation for the common purpose of achieving company goals.

The Japanese system of industrial relations has nourished industrial harmony. As in West Germany, damaging strikes are rare. However, the most persuasive evidence of the positive relationship between productivity and employee participation comes from the quality control circles. With the establishment of these circles, responsibility for quality control shifted from engineers with limited shop-floor experience to employees working in teams with engineers. Numerous examples have been cited of employee suggestions that, when implemented, improved productivity.[7]

It has also been suggested that because of the quality control circles, Japanese workers accept changes in the production process more willingly than workers in environments where solutions are handed down by management. This is particularly important in consumer durable industries, where changes in models require frequent alterations in the production process. Quality control circles also have an impact on the efficiency of production. Because far fewer inspectors are needed, one layer of bureaucracy is substantially reduced. For example, Japanese auto assembly plants have one inspector for every twenty employees; in the United States the ratio is one in seven. Moreover, because there is greater confidence that components are not defective (suppliers, too, are required to achieve rigorous quality standards), many companies can keep minimal inventories. As a result, the need for stock rooms and warehousing is reduced, production costs are lower, and the efficiency of assembly-line operations is increased.

The Japanese system reportedly promotes productivity in other ways. Lifetime employment, although it covers only employees of large firms, or about one-third of the work force, has been credited with reducing employee resistance to the introduction of new technology; workers have cooperated with management in seeking ways to increase productivity without fear of designing themselves out of a job. Lifetime employment has also encouraged employers to invest heavily in the training and retraining of their employees, which has been reported to enhance the overall technical ability of the nation's work force.

Blaming Management

Much of the literature on linking worker participation with productivity growth has focused on harnessing workers' ideas and efforts to perform more effectively. The standard underlying assumption for many American productivity models has been that managers are adequately motivated and need no advice to improve their performance. More recently, however, students of organizational behavior have shifted their attention to examining how employer actions promote or retard productivity growth.

Again using West Germany and Japan as comparative examples, analysts have found that employers in the United States do not provide as much training for their employees as do their counterparts abroad. In West Germany about half the youth leave school at age fifteen or sixteen. Most of these youngsters are admitted to a three-year apprenticeship system provided by employers. This pattern reportedly produces a work force with a high level of technical competency. It also results in low unemployment among young people, in contrast to the U.S. experience. Employers are also willing to provide necessary retraining because they have found that apprentices tend to adapt well to different work environments.[8]

In Japan, employer investments in training are substantial. Many workers are recruited directly from high schools, before they have had a chance to acquire specific job-related skills. Once in the company, they undergo training not only to perform particular tasks but also to prepare them for other jobs in the company.[9]

In the United States, the pattern of individual employment is generally one of changing employers while remaining in the same occupation. The Japanese approach, however, has two implications for productivity; flexible deployment of human resources and acceptance by employees of technological change. Because the employee is trained for the company rather than for the job, narrow occupational lines are obliterated. Also, due to job security in large firms, resistance on the part of employees to technological changes and burdensome work rules is not as pronounced in Japan as in the United States. In the United States, employers do provide considerable resources to employee training, estimated by the American Society for Training and Development to have amounted to about $7 billion in 1983.[10] However, in contrast to the West German and Japanese systems, the bulk of the training effort has focused on management and technical personnel; programs for manual workers are much rarer.

Some analysts fault American employers for their short-term perspective, claiming that it adversely affects the long-term performance of companies.[11] Such short-term perspective is said to be a function of the high rate of turnover among managers and of management's preoccupation with immediate profits. Because managers are often rewarded with bonuses or other forms of compensation largely on the basis of short-term profits, it is argued that they fail to plan and develop strategies for the long run. For example, capital invested in the upgrading of plants and equipment may reduce paper profits in the short run, while acquisition of established companies may result in immediate gains regardless of the long-run effects. Others fault managers who have financial or legal backgrounds for their limited grasp of the production process and for their consequent misallocation of the investments that are needed to improve productivity over the longer term.

American companies tend to approach sales through market research and company response to customer complaints. Attention is devoted to the current demands of customers in an effort to increase sales quickly. This process may frequently result in sacrificing product quality, and quality affects productivity in subtle but direct ways: through reduced waste of materials in the production process and reduced frequency of recalls to fix defective parts.[12]

American managers have also been criticized for failing to motivate production workers. They do not work as closely with those on the shop floor as their Japanese or West German counterparts do, and there are often many layers of bureaucracy between workers and managers. The separation of employees and managers is reinforced by the wide salary differential of American managers and blue-collar workers, a differential which exceeds comparable pay differences abroad. And, as proponents of workers' participation would argue, American managers are less likely to provide channels for meaningful communication and involvement. Consequently, American workers are much less likely to identify with company goals than are employees abroad.

A Model from Abroad?

Even if American labor-management relations have serious deficiencies and the problems are compounded by inappropriate management incentives and objectives, it does not follow that a system which is effective in a foreign country would necessarily prove effective if it were exported to the United States. The fact is that industrial relations are most often shaped by the larger cultural forces that mold a society. The style of American management and the tenor of U.S. industrial relations are deeply embedded in the values and traditions of our society and cannot be readily altered.

Despite the success that has been attributed to the Japanese and West German systems of worker participation and the advocacy of these systems by observers in this country, they are unlikely to proliferate here. In West Germany, as elsewhere in Europe, worker participation is viewed in political terms as an extension of democracy which grants workers the right to participate in the organization that employs them. Such motivation is largely absent from the American labor movement, which is less doctrinaire and tends to focus more on bread-and-butter issues of pay, benefits, and working conditions.

The West Germans' acceptance of the notion of workers' rights to participate in management decisions has been fostered by the relatively high unionization rates across the economy together with the strong political affiliations of the unions. Collective bargaining in European countries tends to be highly centralized, and it is often carried out on an industry-wide basis. Consequently, until worker's councils were established, there was little scope for worker participation at the company level. In contrast, bargaining at the plant level is characteristic of American industrial relations.

The idea of direct participation by labor representatives in corporate management has not been well received by either American management or labor. It has been rejected by managers concerned with their loss of control and by many union leaders who fear losing bargaining effectiveness through shared responsibility. Glenn E. Watts, president of the Communication Workers of America, put the union position succinctly: "I don't want to sit on the board and be responsible for managing the business. I want to be free as a unionist to criticize management."[13]

Although most of organized labor also seems to prefer this adversarial relationship, the one prominent example of codetermination in the United States also reflects the trade union dilemma. In response to their dire economic circumstances and the union "give-backs," the Chrysler Corporation invited the president of the United Auto Workers, Douglas Fraser, to serve on its board of directors so as to improve labor-management relations during a difficult restructuring period. While this arrangement may have worked well for some time, it came to an end abruptly when Chrysler workers failed to agree on a new contract. Fraser resigned from the board before renegotiation of the contract began, citing conflict of interest (though he later returned after the contract had been signed). This would not happen in the West

German context because bargaining is centralized and labor representatives seated on company boards are proscribed by law from participating in collective bargaining. Apart from these legal and organizational distinctions, it is clear that the leaders of American labor unions are wary of being co-opted by management in matters they perceive to be of doubtful advantage to themselves or to their members.

It is equally unlikely that the Japanese model of worker participation would be readily accepted in the United States, despite the outpouring of articles from business schools and assorted experts praising superior Japanese labor-management relations. Again, management seems to be opposed to diluting its authority through consensus decisionmaking. Perceiving the process to be slow and cumbersome, American management tends to regard these practices as inimical to efficiency. The difficulty is that Japanese practices are foreign to American culture and traditions. Consensus decisionmaking in Japan derives from a system of hierarchical relations governed by a paternalism in which the leader is responsible for all members of the group. Worker participation in Japan is integral to that country's unique system of industrial relations. Lifetime employment, seniority wages, and enterprise unions interact to harmonize individual and company goals, thereby laying the foundation on which meaningful communication and participation can be built.

Whatever the merits of the much-publicized Japanese system of industrial relations, it applies only to large companies, which employ about one-third of the work force.[14] This leaves a sizable secondary labor market of women and temporary workers who have little or no say in the terms and conditions of their work or in the management decisions that affect them.

No doubt, if advocates of overhauling American industrial relations had their way, some impediments to productivity growth would be removed. Adoption of the desired reform must be preceded, however, by a change of attitudes. Large-scale borrowing from successful practices abroad does not seem likely, nor could these practices be easily adopted. Traditions, norms, and legal arrangements differ too much among countries for such practices to be imported, as the limited success of experimental U.S. programs tends to demonstrate.

Quality-of-Work-Life Experiments

Major portions of foreign industrial relations models may not be transferrable to the American context, but experiments have been undertaken to implement some salient features from the foreign models. Quality-of-work-life programs became a growth industry in the United States during the 1970s. These experiments fit better with U.S. traditions than the more legalistic West German or culturally different Japanese approaches. Advocates asserted that work reform—either through job enrichment or participatory management—would make jobs more satisfying and would usher in a new era of labor-management cooperation. This, in turn, would lead to increased productivity. In the inflationary, high-interest environment of the 1970s, the idea of investing in participatory management as a means to improve productivity proved attractive.

The results of these experiments are far from conclusive. Several studies have reported the experiences of some 200 American corporations experimenting with quality-of-life programs. These ranged from changes in individual job design (enlargement, rotation, or enrichment) to more sophisticated meshings of technology and group-work design (the sociotechnical approach). On the basis of these experiments, proponents were quick to claim that the quality-of-work-life movement was gaining momentum. The hope, expressed or implied, was that encouraging employees to participate in decisions that affect their day-to-day work patterns would lead to an increase in their productivity. Drawing upon their creativity and expertise in helping to redesign jobs and improve the efficiency of the work process also would enhance productivity.

Despite all the claims surrounding the establishment of these programs there is little persuasive evidence that changes in the work environment improve productivity. According to a Work in America

Institute report summarizing the literature on productivity and quality-of-work-life programs in the 1970s, "In isolated situations improved quality of work life can result in increases in productivity. We cannot, however, surmise that this is a direct cause-effect relationship."[15] A New York Stock Exchange study was equally inconclusive. It reported that corporations which had established worker participation or related programs used them sparingly and that the programs involved only a fraction of the corporations' employees.[16] Expressing hope for the future, the researchers suggested that human-resource programs might eventually be effective in raising productivity, but they noted that most of the programs covered by their study had been in place for only two years or less, and thus many may have been producing a short-run improvement that would be difficult to sustain—the familiar Hawthorne effect of producing short-term gains that quickly evaporate. Although some U.S. companies have recently been highly successful in this area, a reliable and adequate sample of corporate experience is hard to come by. Firms are not prone to report failures, and researchers are dependent upon company-released data that generally put experiments in the best possible light.

The real problem with establishing meaningful worker participation programs that contribute to greater productivity is that they require a redistribution of power within the workplace.[17] The traditional management perspective is that the retention of control and final decisionmaking authority is essential to profit maximization. Although some employers may seek the advice of their employees in order to solve production problems, management in general is more likely to want workers to "feel" involved rather than actually help to make policy. For this reason, American management has established very modest objectives for worker participation.

It is also not clear that American workers want far-reaching changes in their work life or that management wants to encourage such changes. To workers, greater productivity may represent a threat to jobs by speeding up the production process or eliminating old and protected ways of doing things. Conversely, management does not generally view greater efforts at improving productivity as a cooperative venture. Rather, it sees the process as one of gaining from labor greater flexibility in job assignment, production standards, crew sizes, and other elements over which labor has gained control as a result of established practices or collective-bargaining agreements.[18]

Labor has been wary of work-reform schemes. Skeptical unionists believe that many experiments at the workplace are designed to raise production standards and thereby to elicit greater work effort and circumvent seniority systems. Unions fear that these initiatives will become a means of avoiding fair compensation and will leave workers no real ability to influence key corporate decisions or to exercise greater control over their work lives. Indeed, compared to experiments abroad, most American programs have been quite limited. In Sweden, where some fundamental changes have been made in traditional assembly-line work, the work process had to be totally reordered in many cases to give workers autonomy, and new pay and profit-sharing systems were devised based on a combination of group and individual effort.

Even the limited cooperation and consultation associated with quality control circles, a concept originally developed in the United States, is viewed with suspicion by American management and unions. Proposals by employees are not readily accepted by supervisors, who are concerned about their loss of authority, or by production engineers, who may have little direct contact with the workers making the suggestions. Consequently, many of the existing American circles tend to provide a more narrow scope for participation and for potential productivity gains. There are, of course, a number of exceptions and a number of reports of successful experiments, but the limited adoption of quality control techniques reflects continued union and management ambivalence toward these programs.[19]

The idea of increasing productivity by means of greater participation at the workplace is deceptively simple. Evidently workers have productive potential that is not being tapped. ''Turning on'' their creative energies would no doubt improve the performance of many companies. Worker participation could also provide the basis for a new spirit of cooperation, which would make it easier for management and labor to set goals and work toward them collectively. In practice, however, the hoped-for reforms run counter to deeply embedded authoritarian norms and American cultural values of individualism and competitive struggle. These values translate into adversarial and hierarchical relations at the workplace.

It is therefore unrealistic to assume that in assessing existing relationships labor and management are going to focus on cooperation and productivity considerations at the expense of traditional interests and motivations. This statement applies not only to situations where relations are governed by collective-bargaining agreements but also in the nonunion sector, where management's power is often greater. Consequently, any effort to encourage greater cooperation will have to focus on working within the traditional system rather than on building parallel but often ephemeral structures.

4

Prospects for the Next Decade

As the first signs of recovery from the worst recession since the 1930s became manifest in 1983, U.S. productivity growth showed some strong increases. Already the economy has experienced a number of encouraging developments as new and more productive technologies have been introduced in factories and offices. Also, demographic trends could favor productivity growth, and as foreign trade becomes increasingly important it may stimulate our economic performance to assure American competitiveness in world markets. However, only if these opportunities can be carefully exploited by appropriate policies will these developments translate into an improvement in American productivity.

New Technologies

One of the greatest potential boosts to productivity in the next decade will be the development and application of scientifically based technologies. Biotechnology and genetic engineering promise tremendous advances in chemicals, medicine, and health care as well as in the production of food. New technologies, just now appearing on the horizon, portend the development of cheaper and more durable types of materials for the construction of cars, houses, factories, and machines. And microelectronics technology has the potential of revolutionizing information-processing and delivery systems and of automating factories, homes, and offices, thereby resulting in higher-quality products and services at lower real prices.

Microelectronics provides the best example of technological advances that currently carry wide applications for numerous parts of the economy in the immediate years ahead.[1] Essentially, microelectronics is the miniaturization of electronic components. It has caused a revolution in computers and their uses. Two decades ago, computers were expensive, slow in processing information, and took up large amounts of space. Because of these characteristics, they were available to only a few large enterprises. Today's computers are an amazing contrast: what filled a room in 1960 can now be held in the palm of one's hand. Cost, speed, and efficiency have been similarly enhanced. A silicon chip one centimeter square now holds a system of integrated circuits that can perform hundreds of thousands of multiplications per second and store about 1,300 words of text. A microprocessor chip that costs $20 today has the computing power of a machine which cost about $1 million two decades ago. If cars had developed as rapidly as computers over the past two decades, a Rolls Royce would cost $2.50 and would run for 600,000 miles on a gallon of gasoline.

Because of reductions in size and cost and increases in speed and accuracy, microelectronics has vastly expanded the applications of computers. At one end of the scale, the microcomputer has taken over tasks that once would have been too expensive to perform electronically. At the other end, computers can now be used to regulate, monitor, and control production processes that were once too complex to be undertaken. Both applications have substantially influenced productivity and reliability.

A few examples illustrate the productivity-enhancing features of microelectronics. In the retail trade the use of scanning equipment has changed the way business is done. Each product is tagged with a code that can be read by a computer through the use of a scanning device, often a laser beam built into the checkout counter. When the code is read, the computer then records its price at the cash register and also notes on the inventory records that this item has been sold. Computerization of retail outlets has brought faster check-out times for customers, particularly in supermarkets, continuously updated inventory records that tell when to restock shelves or reorder goods, and detailed sales for the company's marketing analysts.

Similarly in banks, the new uses of the computer have allowed customers to access their accounts instantly, deposit money, and make cash withdrawals through automatic teller machines which at the same time make the appropriate updates to the account. This has substantially curtailed the time spent on paperwork in most banks and has allowed them to expand their services into other areas. The machine, unlike human workers, does not complain about being a "twenty-four-hour" teller.

Word processors (typewriters with a memory) are perhaps the best-known type of computer-based office equipment. A word processor facilitates the preparation of written material by capturing the text input in an electromagnetic memory bank. Material can be retrieved from these magnetic cards, tapes, or disks and reproduced, like the music from a record or a tape, as many times as necessary to allow changes, corrections, and revisions. Because material needs to be typed only once, and can be corrected quickly, documents can be produced much faster than with typewriters.

In the factory, microelectronics is increasingly being applied to the design and manufacturing of products. Computer-assisted design (CAD) enables technicians to work on visual display units rather than on traditional drawing boards. This allows errors to be corrected or alternatives to be tried with relative ease, thereby speeding up the process of engineering design considerably. Computer-assisted manufacturing (CAM) is used to smooth out the production process by providing instant information on ordering cycles, work in process, and inventory.

The use of microprocessors in the factory is best illustrated by robots. These mechanical arms can be programmed to perform a variety of tasks ranging from those that are relatively straightforward, such as welding and spray painting, to more complex jobs such as carburetor assembly. Because they can be reprogrammed, they allow rapid conversion of the machines to produce new models or products.

The application of new technologies can also transform the service industries. Software packages that can, for example, present multicolor graphics, translate notes into music, or make interactive instruction possible have the promise of enhancing education, training, and other services.[2] A vast array of educational lessons, vocational training packages, and testing systems already exists. Evaluations have shown that learning—reading, mathematics, vocational skills, occupational information—can be accelerated by individualized, self-paced instruction and computer-managed testing. Computer-assisted instruction can also be effectively used for occupational counseling, job-search assistance, and many other functions that are central to most human-resource services. In hospitals, microelectronics has made available a wide range of diagnostic services and monitoring devices that have increased the efficiency of hospital care.

As microelectronic technology advances, its applications will become even more widespread. This is occurring on several fronts. Chips are becoming smaller—that is, the number of integrated circuits on each chip is increasing dramatically—allowing more information to be processed per second. While it is impossible for today's computers to fully simulate a particular airplane's performance at the design stage, advances in chip technology, now in the experimental stages, should make this a reality in this decade. The results will be a substantial reduction in work time and vastly improved productivity in aircraft design and manufacture. Other innovations, such as voice-sensitive computers that can directly transcribe dictation into written texts, may be marketable in the not too distant future.

Perhaps the most significant development in microelectronics, however, is the convergence of the computer with telecommunications. While the telephone network has for some years allowed not only voice but also data transmission, advances in the form of digital exchanges that use the same transmitting mode as computers will greatly speed up communications and make them cheaper and more accurate. The replacement of copper wires with optical fibers that use pulses of light to transmit information allows more messages to be carried simultaneously, making two-way television economical and thus opening the gates to the more widespread use of interactive television screens.

Satellite communications offer another promising technology for transmitting information. Some large U.S. companies are already providing their own communication services or selling the use of a network to other companies. Such systems offer instant delivery of documents and ultra high speed data transmission. This technology has enabled the *Wall Street Journal*, the *New York Times*, and *USA Today* to be produced and distributed on a national and even a world-wide basis. Cables of optical fibers are also used to link offices in a network with each other. Information packets are moved around, as though on a conveyor belt, and each office has a device to determine if a package is addressed to it.

These systems represent the basic elements of the integrated electronic office where each piece of equipment is linked electronically to others. Word processors in New York can send messages instantaneously to a linked processor in London or can be interfaced with phototypesetting equipment or electronic filing systems. Thus, vendors now advertise integrated work stations where a single operator can move from checking invoices to editing documents or revising data files.

By expediting the handling of information, microelectronics enhances the productivity not only of clerical workers but also of managers—those who generate, analyze, coordinate, and interpret information. Similarly, in factories, the productivity of assembly-line workers is augmented by robots, while the most skilled engineers use sophisticated tools to increase their effectiveness.

Constraints?

As with most other technological advances, the promises of computer technology also raise concern about technologically induced unemployment. In factories, production workers and their immediate

61

supervisors are most likely to be affected by these changes, while in offices, those performing clerical tasks such as bookkeeping, filing, typing, and other information-handling activities are more likely to be at risk. And in addition to the potential for labor displacement, these jobs are likely to undergo substantial change as skill requirements are altered, traditional career paths are significantly modified, and the way in which the work itself is done undergoes transformation.

Of course, contrary to some gloomy forecasts, changes in the number of jobs and in the character of work are not likely to occur overnight. For one thing, despite the potential for rapid diffusion, in practice there are a number of constraints that have slowed the pace of change and that are likely to continue to do so. The adoption of technological improvements is dependent upon potential cost savings and the level of required investment. Where the new technology requires substantial redesigning of plants or production processes (e.g., the introduction of robots in manufacturing), or where the capital tied up in plant is very high (as in the steel industry), the rate of diffusion is likely to be slow. Also, in cases in which older structures are not equipped for the new technology and would require costly remodeling before the new technology could be introduced, these higher costs may impede adoption of the new equipment. Projections of a jobless future under a new technology often ignore these economic realities.

In the service sector, which is thinly capitalized compared with manufacturing, the diffusion of technology is expected to be much more rapid. In the past, many analysts believed that a larger service sector would seriously restrict an economy's ability to boost output per inputs. Yet microelectronic and other advances appear to be eliminating some production constraints. However, management's lack of awareness of potential applications as well as innate resistance to change and probable shortages of appropriately skilled personnel will tend to restrain change.[3]

Attitudes also play a restraining role. Acceptance of new technology in the office may be delayed until executives learn to enter and extract information from the system. Also, managers and clerical workers alike frequently resist the organizational changes implied by the new office systems, fearing loss of status and loss of interpersonal relations with their colleagues. Customer attitudes also play a constraining role. Long accustomed to face-to-face encounters at the bank teller's window or the reservations counter, customers resist impersonal service from machines. For this reason many companies that pride themselves on personalized service avoid the introduction of new equipment. In the service sector, then, the spread of new technology is likely to occur gradually as the equipment itself becomes more sophisticated and easy to use, as costs continue to fall, and as both the work force and the public become acclimated to the changed environment.

Acceptance of a changing work environment and job content will likely increase the need for greater job security both within the companies themselves and in the economy as a whole. Almost two decades ago, a presidential commission that was established to review the impact of the first wave of computer technology on jobs concluded: "The basic fact is that technology eliminates jobs not work."[4] This assessment, of course, implies the need for a flexible labor force which has access to training to develop the skills that will enable workers to take new jobs within companies or elsewhere in the economy.

The new technologies that are already available in the marketplace and that are emerging from research laboratories have the potential to enhance productivity across the economy in this decade and beyond. Realization of this potential, however, requires a stable economic environment to encourage investments, and a growing economy so that gains in productivity do not translate into labor displacement. It also requires a skilled work force and occupational safeguards that will encourage the acceptance of change in work places and in the economy as a whole. These, in turn, will require some significant changes in both public and private policies.

A More Mature Labor Force

Between 1975 and 1979 the U.S. labor force grew at an average annual rate of 2.7 percent. Even during the years of high unemployment between 1980 and 1983, the work force continued to grow, although at a slower rate, 1.5 percent. The Bureau of Labor Statistics projects that this growth rate will decline to 1.1 percent in the second half of the 1980s.[5] During the same period the number of young people between the ages of sixteen and twenty-four is expected to fall by at least 1.5 million, reducing their proportion of the labor force from 24 percent in 1975 to 18.4 percent by the end of this decade. By definition this means that the labor force will be more mature than it has been in the past.

Whether an older work force translates into a more productive one is uncertain. Of course, the "baby boom" generation is better educated, in terms of years of schooling, than its older counterparts. However, many at the upper end of the age spectrum were educated and trained before the spread of computer technology and may lack the skills essential to performing most jobs in the coming years. This is especially true for many women, who are expected to account for two of every three additions to the labor force in the 1980s. According to the BLS, women are much less likely than men to acquire a mathematical background and associated technical skills in their secondary and college education or to acquire these skills in post-secondary vocational preparation.[6] Although there are some signs that this pattern may be changing, the vast majority of women still receive traditional education and training.

The skill gap may be exacerbated by a reversal of the trend toward earlier retirement as changes in the social security and private pension systems postpone retirement. Older workers tend to learn new skills less easily and to have more difficulties adjusting to changing circumstances.

A highly educated work force may have a more indirect and perverse impact on productivity if workers are over qualified for their employment opportunities. During the 1970s highly educated workers performed essentially the same functions as had their less well schooled predecessors.[7] The share of sales and clerical workers with college degrees nearly doubled during this period, as did the percentage of blue-collar and service workers with one or more years of college. The median educational level attained by the labor force as a whole included a smattering of college-level education. While it is recognized that educated workers have an advantage in coming to grips with technological change, it is also true that more schooling raises expectations for higher earnings and more challenging jobs. This sets the stage for disillusionment if such opportunities do not emerge. Job satisfaction surveys have identified longer schooling and low pay as the key elements of dissatisfaction at work, which may result in disruptive behavior among workers and impact adversely upon productivity.

A more mature work force will be more security conscious. Young workers generally spend their first few years in the labor market job-hopping in an attempt to find the ''right'' spot. As they age, settle down into marriage, and raise families, their working life also tends toward greater stability. Income and job security become more important concerns. Consequently, the aging of the work force is likely to be accompanied by some resistance to change unless it is coupled with greater economic security.

Finally, although the overall birth rate for the United States has been declining, the fertility rates of black and other minority groups have continued to exceed those of whites. Consequently, representation of these groups in the labor force will increase in the 1980s. Historically, unemployment among minority teen-agers has been disturbingly high—as high as 50 percent of the black teen-age labor force—and their labor force participation has been discouragingly low—about 40 percent. Only one in five is employed. Moreover, although they have become increasingly better educated, young minority entrants still tend to have fewer skills and less education than young white entrants. Without significant efforts to develop their skills and to use them productively, these young people are not likely to be either a source or a beneficiary of productivity gains.

The changing composition of the work force can be a positive element for productivity change, but only if participants are equipped with the skills they need to enter the computer age and if they are confident that change can be beneficial rather than punitive.

The Growing Importance of International Trade

Until the 1960s the United States depended largely on its own abundant natural resources and on its large and rich domestic markets. With the rise in production and incomes in other countries following World War II, the United States has increasingly sought to market its goods abroad. By 1982 U.S. exports accounted for 11.5 percent of the nation's GNP, or double the rate of 1960. The Commerce Department has estimated that in the late 1970s one in seven factory jobs was dependent on exports.

U.S. agriculture is even more dependent upon exports. A third of the nation's farming acreage is devoted to growing food that is consumed abroad. And the service sector, which has been growing rapidly, now accounts for an estimated 20 percent of world trade with the United States. International trade and the growth of multinational companies doing business around the globe have had the effect of strengthening the interdependence of national economies.

The United States stands to gain much from continued growth in world trade, yet the outlook is clouded both here and abroad by the growth of protectionist sentiment. U.S. trade policy has been comparatively pro–free trade, as indicated by the reduction in our tariff barriers from about 26 percent in 1946 to about 8 percent in 1978. Yet America has come to rely increasingly upon nontariff barriers—particularly in steel and motor vehicles—to reduce competitive pressures from abroad. These pressures originated partly from the world recession in the early 1980s, which encouraged foreign producers to export merely to prevent their plants' output from falling to uneconomic levels. Another factor is the imbalance in exchange rates that was brought on by the overvaluation of the dollar in the early 1980s relative to the currencies of Western Europe and Japan. Finally, the United States no longer enjoys a comparative advantage in the production of some goods and services. The Japanese can build cars and ship them to U.S. markets more cheaply than Detroit can produce cars for domestic consumption. Given the overvalued dollar, the West Germans can sell high-quality precision tools in the United

States at a lower price than it would cost American manufacturers to produce them domestically.

Some of the reasons for increased foreign competition will recede in the future if stability and growth are restored to the U.S. economy. Because the influence of the United States on world economic conditions is substantial, expansion of the American economy will likely lead to higher world demand and thereby to an increase in exports both here and abroad.

However, restoring growth and stability to the world economy and reducing the exchange value of the dollar will not fully eliminate the pressures of foreign competition on the U.S. economy. The Council of Economic Advisers has suggested that U.S. industries producing steel, motor vehicles, and fuels are presently at a comparative disadvantage in world trade. In contrast, research-intensive manufacturing, as well as producer services, with their above-average levels of growth and productivity advances, enjoy a competitive advantage in world markets.[8]

The productivity performance of the U.S. economy as a whole will benefit from increasing specialization in those goods and services in which the United States has a comparative advantage. This means, however, that some sectors will grow and others will shrink as resources are reallocated among industries and occupations in the economy. Like the changes brought about by the introduction of new technologies, trade may displace many workers, leading to skill mismatches and occupational and geographical adjustment problems. This can involve substantial economic and social costs. It has been estimated that in 1983 some $29 billion will be spent on unemployment insurance for jobless workers, some of whom lost their jobs as a result of foreign competition. And communities that have lost industries face declining tax bases as well as a reduction in social capital.

Clearly, many factors will influence the productivity performance of the United States in the 1980s. The challenge for the American economy is to accommodate and adapt to change and not to deter the expansion of industries that have the potential for growth in productivity and the ability to compete in world markets. Postponing change may, at best, alleviate adversity, but it is not a solution for declining industries. High unemployment remains a key obstacle to acceptance of the essential changes.

PART II

Policy Options

5

Less or More Government

A cornerstone of the Reagan administration's economic policy is the belief that cuts in federal taxes, reductions in domestic spending, and a reining in of regulatory interventions hold the key to a better productivity performance. However, despite the productivity improvements that normally follow a recession, there are indications that Reaganomics has generated several forces that will adversely affect productivity in the long run. Some observers believe that the United States needs an explicit industrial policy to spur growth in leading industries and to help others regain their competitive edge. However, proponents have failed to agree on the ingredients of such a policy. Sometimes overlooked in these debates are steps that could be taken to promote long-term economic stability.

The Supply-Side Approach

In 1981 the Reagan administration advocated comprehensive economic and institutional measures aimed at bolstering productivity growth. Assuming that inadequate capital investment was responsible for the nation's poor productivity performance, administration policymakers attributed the shortage of capital largely to the government's sapping incentives via its tax and spending policies. Excessive government regulation also was pointed to as a factor shackling free enterprise.

The policy response to this diagnosis was to use tax policy to stimulate productivity and economic growth, paying for the loss in tax revenues by cutting nondefense spending. As finally enacted, the "reforms" offered tax relief to high-income taxpayers while reductions in transfer payments left many low-income individuals and families worse off.[1] The Reagan administration justified favoring the affluent on the basis that these tax cuts were consistent with the restoration of productivity growth because the propensity to save is higher among affluent individuals and families than among those with low incomes. It followed, according to the supply-siders, that reductions in the marginal rates of taxes not only would boost savings and investment but would also encourage greater work effort among high-income earners. A different criterion was applied to the poor. A more stringent means test was established to discourage malingering and to induce those presumably able to work to seek employment.

The cuts in business taxes were proportionally more substantial than reductions in personal taxes and were also aimed to stimulate new investment. Prior to their enactment, business tax relief had centered on equipment, with the result that there was little in the way of incentive to invest in new facilities.[2] The government recognized, however, that investment in modern equipment also would require building new plants in order to fully realize the beneficial impacts. Consequently, the Reagan program covered both structures and equipment under its new treatment, which allowed faster depreciation of assets and a more generous tax credit. Taken together, the reductions in personal and business taxes were expected to provide substantial stimulus to the economy. The gains were expected to more than offset the loss of revenues (the so-called supply-side impact), and the benefits were supposed to trickle down to all segments of society.

Claiming that federal government regulations were another major contributor to the productivity slowdown, the Reagan administration favored an overall relaxation in enforcing existing regulations; the transfer of some enforcement authority to state governments; and withdrawal and revision of regulations that mainly affected the auto industry.

On the spending front, the Reagan program's stated intention was to balance the federal budget by retrenching entitlement programs. The net result, however, was an increase in the federal budget and deficit because boosts in military spending and reductions in tax revenues more than offset reductions in social spending. By 1983 the federal debt accounted for 41 percent of the GNP, compared with 34 percent during the four pre-Reagan years, and the estimated annual federal deficit had risen to some $200 billion.

Neither Efficiency nor Equity

Under Reaganomics, the largest share of the benefits has gone to upper-income groups and corporations while the largest burden of the spending cuts has fallen on lower-income groups, particularly the working poor. By providing incentives for some and by freeing the market to operate unfettered by government intrusion, the program attempted to promote a more effective use of resources. In effect, notions of equity and fairness were, at best, of lower priority and, at worst, incompatible with notions of efficiency. In part because of this, the Reagan program, in theory, suffered from some conceptual conflicts, and, in practice, the package that was enacted produced a number of economic tensions that resulted in a short-run net loss of aggregate economic benefits rather than the intended gains. A similar result appeared to be in the offing for the long term.

A fundamental key to increased economic efficiency under the Reagan program was the promotion of savings, investment, and work effort by reducing personal and corporate taxes. Conceptually, a reduction in taxes can have a favorable impact on savings by encouraging future rather than current consumption. In turn, the increased savings can be expected to flow into productive investment. At the same time, reducing taxes can be expected to lower work disincentives that result from progressively higher taxes paid on each dollar earned. In fact, these linkages may not be as straightforward as simple economic theories indicate.

In principle, a tax cut can increase the amount of personal saving by increasing the after-tax rate of return on savings. Evidence on this is inconclusive, however, with some studies suggesting a large impact and others finding no effect at all.[3] The gross rate of savings in the United States has been relatively stable since the end of World War II despite various tax changes, which suggests that it might prove difficult to alter the rate of savings. While Americans might look somewhat wistfully at their thrifty counterparts abroad, who regularly save at rates two to three times as great as savers in the United States, behavioral and institutional differences may account for the savings differentials. Individuals in other nations save at higher rates despite higher tax rates and more comprehensive welfare systems. Among the twenty-four OECD countries, the United States is ranked fourteenth in tax burdens.[4] Most West European countries (but not the Japanese) have a much more elaborate and comprehensive social welfare system and hence are not as dependent on savings for medical emergencies or economic distress. America is and remains a nation of dedicated consumers. In the United States to a much greater extent than in other countries, public and private policies provide incentives to buy: from the mass media exhorting households to spend to the subsidies to buy which are implicit in the tax relief allowed on consumer installment debts and home mortgages.

Tax reductions are also expected to boost investment because a cut in taxes raises the rate of return on such spending. However, if the added investment is not targeted in productive channels, then raising aggregate investment does not necessarily improve economic efficiency. Under the Reagan program, the investment incentives were applied to speculative and unproductive investments as well as to investments in new plant and equipment. Moreover, because it focused tax relief on depreciable assets rather than on corporate income tax rates, the program tended to favor goods-producing industries rather than less capital-intensive services and small, high-technology companies, where there is substantial potential to increase productivity.

With respect to the impact of taxes on work effort, the Reagan program was based on the explicit assumption that individual behavior differs according to income level. The tax cuts were expected to bring forth extra effort from the relatively well-off groups, while the increased tax burden on the working poor was not expected to reduce their work efforts. Most studies suggest that among prime-aged men, work effort, as measured by the number of hours worked in a year, is not affected by changes in wage rates or, by implication, by changes in tax rates. For women, the response has been found to be different, in part because home activities, though unremunerated, represent an alternative use of time.[5] The working poor, having lost a substantial portion of their benefits, were expected to work harder to replace those losses with additional earnings. This expectation ignores both the incentives affecting these individuals and their circumstances. For many low-income individuals, extra earnings over a broad range are taxed at rates greater than 100 percent (and even greater if loss of Medicaid eligibility is included). There is clearly nothing in the way of an incentive to work in these circumstances, which means, in effect, that society does not care if these people work or not. And yet it is clearly a negation of efficiency rules to leave a proportion of the population in a poverty trap from which it is difficult to escape.

Furthermore, the escape route has been narrowed by the Reagan program's substantial cutbacks in employment and training funds. Participation in these programs was found to be associated with higher postenrollment earnings, which suggests that these investments had some positive impact on productivity.[6] The administration's rationale for cutting the training programs and eliminating public service jobs was that the unskilled would benefit from the resulting economic growth and that no further effort on their behalf was worth the costs. However, others have pointed out that employment and training programs "form the necessary spout through which economic prosperity trickles down to such people."[7] Over time, then, it is likely that such cuts not only will increase deprivation among the working poor but also will cost society in lost productivity and probably in increased welfare dependency. Limiting the funding available for education and lessening direct aid to students also are likely to reduce the opportunities of children from disadvantaged homes to escape poverty.

Other parts of the Reagan program may have adverse effects on the nation's overall productivity as well. The military build-up is one example. Defense expenditures are expected to rise from 4.6 percent of the GNP, the level prevailing in early 1980, to about 7.3 percent in 1987. The main consequence of this increase in defense spending has been to add to the budget deficit, swelling it to the point where private investors may be crowded out of the money market and thus jeopardizing the much-needed boost in capital spending.

In the system of contracting for new products, there is little incentive to produce in a cost-effective way because cost "overruns" are more or less routinely funded. Also, the spin-offs of defense technology to civilian sectors are diminishing as highly specialized defense needs restrict potential applications to nondefense activities.[8] At a time when industry's need to increase investments in research and development is important, rising military expenditures may divert technically trained personnel from industrial to military applications because it is difficult for industry to compete with contractors working on cost-plus federal contracts.

The Impact of Reaganomics

If some of the administration's key policies have had rather different effects on the nation's productivity over time than was expected, their implementation certainly has been instrumental in bringing on the most severe recession of the post–World War II period. Despite some recovery from recession lows, projected budget deficits and lingering high real interest rates may crimp a sustained long-term comeback. President Reagan's objectives of reducing inflation and unemployment while stimulating productivity growth do not differ from the goals of most of his predecessors. However, the policy mix of monetary restraint and untested supply-side theories has achieved one of the objectives at tremendous cost to another. It has also produced a budget deficit that threatens to undermine some of the gains made on the inflation front or to reduce substantially the amount of loanable funds available to investors. Both scenarios have adverse implications for productivity.

Reaganomics cannot then be judged a success in providing a satisfactory long-term solution to the productivity problem. Overall, performance worsened in the short term because of the recession, high real rates of interest, and uncertainties about inflation, all of which have depressed business investments. Over the longer term, an increase in investment in physical capital stock would have to be balanced against the reductions of investments in human resources. Leaving aside the question of equity as a policy goal, it is probable that the efficiency objectives of the Reagan program have not been met because of the adverse consequences of cutbacks in education, training, work experience, and basic social services.

More fundamentally, the program's aim of changing the institutional environment by reducing the role of government is of questionable value to longer-term economic performance. The notion that the trickle down effect of economic growth is the best way to ensure equal sharing of the benefits will remain an unfulfilled promise, as experience has shown time and again in this country and abroad. The resulting inherent tensions would necessarily adversely influence the future course of the economy.

The economic recession in the early 1980s has had adverse effects on productivity because the poor business climate produced no incentives to invest in new plants or equipment. In real terms, business investment spending fell as tax incentives were swamped by the impact of sluggish conditions and high real interest rates. This is also likely to adversely affect the near-term productivity picture.

Some have claimed that U.S. businesses emerged from the 1981–1982 recession "leaner and fitter," better able to compete in the market as the economy recovered. However, data on business

77

costs do not support this proposition. Payroll costs have, of course, fallen due to layoffs, but other budget items were not substantially trimmed. The number of executive, managerial, and administrative employees continued to increase during the recession. Although it is true that the recession was accompanied by a sharp rise in the number of bankruptcies, it is by no means clear that this was a case of survival of the fittest. Many of the companies that went under were new or small, and were dependent on credit for working capital. They failed under a burden of debt, not necessarily because they were less productive than those that survived. In contrast, many mature and less-productive firms had better access to capital markets and on more favorable terms. Finally, the 4 percent productivity spurt that occurred during the first half of 1983 should not be cause for complacency. Such an increase is a normal cyclical phenomenon that accompanies economic recovery. The test will come when the recovery matures and employers begin to rehire workers. Unless new investments are undertaken or the labor force acquires new skills, the boost in productivity may not be sustained.

Industrial Policy

In the wake of the failure of laissez faire ("less government") policies to promote productivity growth, leading Democrats and others have proposed a more active government role. Advocates of a national industrial policy argue that market forces work too slowly and sometimes in inappropriate directions. Proponents of an activist policy cite the higher rates of productivity growth attained in Japan, West Germany, and France as evidence of the effectiveness of government policies that channel resources into productive activities.

Foreign Experience

Industrial policies in these countries generally share the objectives of channeling economic activities to progressively higher value-added sectors and discouraging less-productive industries. Public policy in Japan has been increasingly directed to provide incentives to high-technology sectors, while more traditional activities such as shipbuilding have been pruned to an efficient scale of production. Similarly, in West Germany the development of innovative production processes and products has been a cornerstone of industrial policy, while the capacity of basic industries such as steel has been reduced to fit changing domestic and world demand.

Although the strategies may be similar, each country has developed its own unique mechanisms for putting theory into practice. In Japan, industrial policy has been developed by the Ministry of International Trade and Industry (MITI), working closely with the business community. MITI has largely focused on enhancing international competitiveness by channeling investment into selected growth industries having potential foreign markets. The French government also relies on centralized planning, West Germany has relied more on market mechanisms, but its banking system has played a unique role in channeling investment funds. The United Kingdom lacks a comprehensive, long-range industrial policy and thus has adopted ad hoc measures in its attempts to save declining industries. As a result, government aid has been directed to many inefficient industries, and the nation's overall productivity growth has declined. The Thatcher government has attempted to abandon these ad hoc arrangements but is still spending billions backing both winners and losers.

These diverse results suggest that positive policies often are successful in efforts to raise productivity, while more defensive and decentralized approaches tend to fail. The industrial policies of Japan, West Germany, France, and the United Kingdom provide a useful summary of the range of policy options open to the United States. Although the experience of these countries cannot be transplanted directly to the United States, the lessons from foreign attempts to channel industrial growth do provide some insights to help shape policy in this country.

Japan. The Japanese government's involvement in directing investment activity dates back to before World War II. In the early stages of recovery from the war, the government adopted a set of

79

policies that were designed to enable the country to catch up with other Western industrialized countries by moving resources into progressively more capital-intensive, high-technology industries. These sectors appeared to be capable of raising real income, accelerating technological progress, and increasing labor productivity. Initially, Japanese policy focused on the development of shipbuilding, steel, power generation, and fertilizer. As economic development advanced, the favored industries included automobiles, chemicals, petrochemicals, and computers. The government's current agenda calls for increasing investment in electronics, telecommunications, new-materials technology, biotechnology, and robotics. By and large, the government's investment in the favored industries has paid off, although some efforts have failed, notably in the aircraft manufacturing industry.

The policies adopted in each case have been formulated under the auspices of the Ministry of International Trade and Industry with the close cooperation of business and government and the acquiescence of Japanese workers. Tax incentives for research and development, accelerated depreciation for targeted industries, government grants, and subsidized loans have been used to promote desired investments and promote structural change. Following the 1973 rise in oil prices, Japan established a credit guarantee fund to help the fertilizer and steel industries (which were most adversely affected by the higher oil prices) adjust to the changed economic circumstances.[9] In contrast, the U.S. reaction to rising oil prices reflected a concern for the needy, and assistance was provided to the poor and elderly for heating their homes.

One facet of Japanese policy is the pooling of company resources to accomplish a specific goal. For example, in the early 1970s MITI suggested that the six largest electronics firms join in a semiconductor research program in which each company would perform designated aspects of the project to avoid duplication. Seed money amounting to $132 million was lent by the government for the project, and repayment was made contingent upon the profitability of the outcome.

Partly as a result of this project, Japan took the lead in the development and manufacture of high-capacity semiconductor chips.

Another important instrument of Japanese industrial policy is credit allocation by government-owned financial institutions and by the commercial banks. What is especially significant here is that in Japan, financial institutions are the chief source of investment funds, while in the United States, companies generate their own investment funds. Also, protectionist trade policies have helped Japanese industries to ward off foreign competition and have allowed new industries to develop.

While tariffs and other protectionist policies have helped Japanese firms, many of their products have faced stiff, domestic competition. Despite its smaller size, Japan's economy supports more auto producers than the United States. Japan's success with industrial policies seems to be based on its pragmatic approach. While mistakes have been made, success has more often been the result.

France. Of all the major industrialized nations, France has had the most explicit industrial policy. During much of the post–World War II period the French government promulgated successive five-year plans which were intended to modernize the nation's industries and make them internationally competitive.[10] Initially, government involvement included direct financing, ownership, and operation of major enterprises. During the 1950s and 1960s, under conservative governments, the instruments of industrial policy were expanded to include price controls, public investment corporations, and credit institutions designed to provide low-cost insurance to industries.

A prime function of French industrial policy has been to allocate resources for economic growth. Pointing to the high rate of growth over the postwar period and to France's rising standard of living, proponents have declared that policy a success. One of the key reasons it worked well during the postwar period was the fact that the French population accepted and supported *dirigisme*—the idea that centralized direction of the economy is desirable. Although consensus-building and cooperation between government, business, and labor were important, government leadership was the chief catalyst and agent of the planning process.

Following the oil crisis of 1973, French policy changed. The government diminished its direct involvement and worked instead through a centralized financial system which controlled virtually all sources of credit. Dismantling the system of controls and subsidies which had existed since the end of World War II, it developed diverse and flexible mechanisms for decisionmaking and implementation in cooperation with financial institutions and the industry groups involved. Once the parties decided on a course of action, financing could follow immediately, and the decision could be implemented rapidly. The aim of industrial policy also changed from the development of national prestige industries such as nuclear power to the promotion of products for international markets, particularly in the fields of electronics, telecommunications, and aerospace.[11] The policy was successful in the latter two industries, but so far it has been quite unsuccessful in electronics; the present government has had to resort to protectionist measures and cash infusions to keep these companies afloat.

France's socialist government, led by François Mitterrand, has attempted to reestablish more centralized planning by nationalizing several large banks and six large companies. However, plans for these companies to serve as engines of growth have apparently gone awry as the government has had to spend billions of francs to prop them up at a time when the nation can least afford it.

West Germany. Industrial policy in West Germany differs from that of Japan and France in that the government does not directly intervene in the investment decisions of industries and firms. Rather, the government has attempted to establish a stable economic climate conducive to investor confidence and has allowed the market to determine the direction of investment. This apparent laissez-faire approach is complemented by government guidance of investment through tax policies and a broad range of industrial aids. For the most part, subsidies have been aimed at helping specific industries rationalize their production in order to become competitive, not at saving jobs or propping up dying industries.[12]

Government policies alone, however, do not capture the flavor of West Germany's industrial policy. The nation's banking system, combined with a cooperative relationship between labor, management, and government, supplies the major mechanisms for policy. As in Japan and France, banks play a major role in directing the flow of funds because companies rely on loaned capital for investment. The power of the private banks derives from the fact that they hold stock in many of the large companies and hence are represented on their boards. Private West German banks also assume a risk-taking role by making long-term corporate loans—a function often undertaken by the governments of France and Japan. Finally, the private banks play the traditional role of providing information about investment, frequently acting indirectly as agents for government policy, particularly for the central Deutsche Bundesbank.

The other key ingredient of West Germany's industrial policy is the close cooperation that exists between government, labor, and management; it is a relationship that permits consensus-building on future directions for policy. At the beginning of the 1970s, a social consensus emerged that if high real wages and incomes were to be maintained, the economy would have to be restructured away from low-skill activities—in which developing countries were establishing a comparative advantage—and toward high-value-added, high-technology industries. Following the 1973 oil shock, energy-efficient production also became an objective. The key to progress on this front was capacity reduction in heavy industries and government support for research and development to stimulate innovation. Rationalization and the reorganization of the advanced-technology sectors, in turn, were aided by the cooperative relationship of management and labor, which is based on codetermination arrangements at the company level. With labor representatives participating in national discussions as well as in company decisions, resistance to change is largely avoided.

The United Kingdom. The industrial policy of the United Kingdom provides a contrasting picture of methods used and results
obtained. Rather than develop policy within the context of an overall
plan or economic goal, as has been the case in Japan, France, and
West Germany, the British set up forty sectoral development committees to analyze what needed to be done to improve productivity
and competitiveness in each sector. Although central direction was to
be given by the National Economic Development Council
(NEDC)—a tripartite body composed of government, labor, and
business—this council did not set priorities for investment projects.
As a result, in the 1970s diverse industrial policy measures were
scattered across the whole spectrum of manufacturing industries.[13]

The lack of central direction meant that in practice, funds were used
to prop up and protect nearly every ailing branch of industry rather
than to reshape the economy toward viable and competitive activities.
Business opposed giving government the power to pick winners,
being wary of how a Labour government would identify a "winner."
Similarly, the idea of letting "losers" go was opposed by the trade
unions and business alike. The government's social and macroeconomic policies often compounded the difficulties by being incon-
sistent or in conflict with plans for strengthening British industry.

In addition to instituting the sectoral industrial policy, the British
have attempted to encourage investment through tax-relief policies
and to direct its flow by providing financial incentives for businesses
to locate and expand in depressed areas. Other forms of government
assistance have included support for industrial innovation (mainly in
the aerospace and nuclear-power industries), direct aid to particular
firms (especially those in the high-technology sector), and national-
ization of the automobile, coal, and steel industries. When the
Thatcher government took over in 1979, the existing industrial policy
fell into disfavor, but today substantial Treasury funds still support
state-owned companies in the high-technology sector as well as the
nationalized industries. Despite the Conservative government's
efforts to "privatize" many of these companies, little progress has
been made.

A Policy for the United States?

Current U.S. industrial policies encompass many ad hoc government actions dealing with defense, taxes, business regulations, immigration, antitrust, job training, and labor relations. Military and space spending have played a major role in the growth of the aerospace, shipbuilding, electronics, and communications industries. Public purchasing tends to favor American-made goods and services. Federal assistance to agriculture in the form of price supports, subsidized loans, and research and development has both protected incomes in this sector and enabled it to become highly competitive in international trade. Industrial exports such as aircraft and electrical generating equipment are financed on favorable terms through the Export-Import Bank, but antitrust regulations hinder American companies from pooling resources to compete in foreign markets. Each of these activities affects the structure of American industry, but they lack a unifying framework for coordinating federal involvement.

Proponents of an industrial policy argue that the lack of a coherent strategy adversely affects economic performance and that government activity should be substantially broadened to counteract market distortions and thereby boost productivity. In theory, it is argued, prices can be relied on to allocate resources in an efficient manner under competitive conditions. In the real world, however, the price mechanism does not always allocate resources effectively, and corrective action based on the cooperative efforts of labor, management, and government often is necessary.

Could a comprehensive industrial policy work in the United States? In the absence of fundamental changes in American institutions and attitudes, success in transplanting all or even major parts of the Japanese or European policies would be highly doubtful. In Japan, France, and West Germany, investments are financed from external sources. Either the government or the banks assume the risks, and this gives them leverage over the decisions made by firms in a direct and immediate way. In the United States such mechanisms do not exist. As noted earlier, investment by American companies is in large part financed out of corporate earnings. Where extensive loans are involved, they typically come from several banks, which not only prevents voluntary, coordinated action among lenders but also in many circumstances makes it illegal.

Of course, the U.S. government could create a large, publicly funded investment bank and authorize it to make loans at concessionary rates of interest to support or subsidize specific activities. Assuming that a mechanism to target investment could be established, effective implementation would still be blocked by the deeply engrained opposition of Americans to accepting direction from a central government. Most American politicians have campaigned on a platform of making government smaller, not larger, even though in practice they have seldom delivered on this promise. Moreover, the relationship between business and government has generally been characterized as adversarial, no matter which party has been in power in the White House or Congress. Except in a national emergency, business and labor have displayed a strong aversion to accepting direction from the government. It is equally improbable that business leaders could agree on the appropriate policies. No doubt, each firm and locality would insist that it should be in the bull's-eye of a targeted industrial policy.

The success of the Japanese and West German policies rests in part on the cooperation of labor, management, and government at the national and enterprise levels. The United Kingdom's failure apparently stems in part from this lack of cooperation and from the consequent inability to build a national consensus for an appropriate policy direction. The U.S. position is far closer to the British one than to the Japanese or the German. At the national level, as well as on the shop floor, relations tend to be adversarial. Indeed, there are now so many special-interest groups, each with competing demands, that it is hard to imagine how a consensus could be built. According to one observer, the decline in the United States' productivity performance is associated with the growing role played by special interests.[14]

Reflecting this lack of consensus, even the advocates of an industrial policy are in disagreement over what *industrial policy* means and which sectors of the economy should receive favorable treatment.

Commenting on the idea, Senator Bill Bradley of New Jersey has stated: "I haven't decided how I feel. . . . Once you get beyond the first two or three sentences, it [industrial policy] becomes difficult to explain in a coherent way." Some see the goal of an industrial policy as the reindustrialization of America, the modernizing of basic manufacturing industries to restore growth. Much of this rhetoric has become an argument for propping up declining industries that are no longer efficient or competitive. It is unrealistic to hope that American producers could recapture past abilities to undersell their present competitors in most industrial products. Leaning against the winds of change would result in subsidizing the inefficient and could lead to costly and unwarranted protectionism. This course carries with it the dangers of higher domestic prices for protected goods, the likelihood of retaliation abroad (which would hurt efficient producers), and lower productivity, and it could eventually cause more widespread job loss.

The economy is moving inexorably from goods-producing to service-producing activities. Some proponents of a national industrial policy consider the appropriate focus to be strengthening the information sector, where the applications of electronics and telecommunications presently provide the United States with a competitive advantage in world markets. They argue that investments should be directed toward the enhancement of technical competence in our work force and in research and development pertaining to new technologies—courses that the Japanese and West Germans in particular seem to be following. As Eli Ginzburg has urged, "Americans must unshackle themselves from the notion, dating back to Adam Smith, that goods alone constitute wealth whereas services are nonproductive and ephemeral. At the same time, they should act on Smith's understanding that the wealth of a nation depends on the skill, dexterity, and knowledge of its people."[15]

It is not at all clear how an industrial policy would help absorb the workers displaced from goods-producing industries. Not every factory mechanic can be turned into a skilled computer technician, and not every steel town can become a high-tech center. While New England managed to regenerate its commercial base after the decline of textile manufacturing, it was a slow and painful process. It is not just the declining communities that suffer. As the displaced workers from labor surplus areas move to growth centers, the social capital of the former goes underutilized while the tax burdens of the more prosperous area rise. The so-called boom towns also face profound adjustment problems in the form of increased congestion, pollution, and crime.[16]

Of course, a comprehensive industrial policy could presumably help declining as well as growing industries. Both the manufacturing and service sectors could benefit from increased selective investments. For the smokestack industries, subsidizing efforts to modernize the production process, streamline the scale of operations, and rationalize inefficient plants and equipment could do much to make parts of these industries more competitive in world markets. Indeed, both the Japanese and West German governments have helped declining industries adjust to new circumstances by encouraging mergers with more-successful companies, by providing short-term subsidies to ensure that rationalization occurs smoothly, and by actively assisting displaced workers. However, the problem that proponents of industrial policies have yet to address is how to determine the criteria for selective investments in smokestack industries. In the United States, where a variety of special-interest groups, each with its pet projects, would be competing for funds, there is a very real danger that resources would be spread too thinly, that projects would be scattered in shotgun fashion rather than within the framework of a targeted approach. In 1961, the Area Redevelopment Act was passed in an effort to provide targeted assistance to a few dozen depressed areas, but the effectiveness of the legislation was thwarted when political pressures expanded eligibility for the assistance to nearly two-thirds of all the counties in the nation. Similarly, the Trade Adjustment Act was turned into a multi-billion-dollar income-support program that provided little funding for the retraining of workers or for making trade adjustments.

In the absence of a national consensus, an effective way to deal with the need for rationalization is to focus on specific circumstances on a case-by-case basis. Many might argue that the special pleading of the Chrysler Corporation should have been ignored. However, if the company had been allowed to fail, the costs would likely have spread beyond the loss of jobs and income to a reduction in the confidence of investors throughout the economy. Focusing on each case would not be incompatible with productivity objectives if loans or guarantees were made contingent upon concessions by all parties to achieve an efficient scale of production.

As far as the information sector is concerned, it seems clear that the key to high productivity and competitiveness lies in investments in research and development. The Japanese example is instructive. The government-supported channeling of five of the largest computer companies' resources into the development of microelectronics has made Japan the world's front runner in the development of high-capacity microchips, the basic building block of tomorrow's more efficient computers. In the United States several large computer companies are mounting a similar research-and-development effort, but without government support they are in danger of running afoul of antitrust laws (which may be the main reason why the largest U.S. computer concern, IBM, has not joined the program).

Despite the lack of agreement on the scope and purpose of a U.S. industrial policy, political interest in the concept has grown considerably. Assuming that the government should play a role in the restructuring of the economy, the obstacles to that restructuring remain formidable, if not insurmountable, in the absence of an institutional environment appropriate to the effort. In the current economic and political climate, there is little room for optimism. Economic conditions will have to deteriorate further before political will and social cohesion can be developed to fashion the policy needed to revitalize the economy.

Incomes Policy

A slack economy, destabilizing inflation, and high interest rates have been the major contributors to the deterioration of U.S. productivity. This fact reflects the inability of policymakers to fight inflation without putting the economy on a roller coaster ride. A tight monetary policy necessarily results in high interest rates, which discourage investment. If, in addition, aggregate demand is weakened, businesses will postpone investment in research on new products or in modernizing plant and equipment. Correspondingly, workers faced with slack labor markets will resist change. The inevitable result is low productivity. Recent experience demonstrates the prohibitive costs of anti-inflation policies that rely excessively upon macroeconomic tools to slow economic activity.

One potentially less costly way of reducing inflation would be an incomes policy that regulates wages and prices. Because payments to labor make up about two-thirds of the cost of production and because costs have a major impact on prices, an incomes policy in theory could deal directly with the sources of inflationary pressures with less adverse effects on the rest of the economy compared to tight monetary or fiscal policies. In the United States such a policy has been tried in various forms several times. In the mid 1960s, wage-price guidelines were established to encourage pay and pricing policies consistent with the growth of productivity. Under the Nixon administration pay and price controls went through several iterations, from freezes to mandatory controls to persuasion. The Carter administration set up voluntary standards and encouraged compliance by appealing to public opinion and threatening the loss of government contracts.

Experience with the various forms of incomes policies tried in the United States has been mixed. Each administration has claimed success in keeping pay and price rises below what they otherwise would have been, but each has also ignored whatever distortions were created and the impact they have had upon economic efficiency. Ideally, policy should attempt to lower the average rate of pay and price increases while allowing specific prices and wages to adjust in response to supply-and-demand conditions. In practice, however, an effective incomes policy must necessarily regulate the wages and prices of individual firms. Over time, the lack of adjustment of relative prices to changing market conditions can lead to distortions and losses in efficiency. In any case, the claimed benefits are relatively short-lived. Once each policy is relaxed, workers attempt to catch up with past increases in the cost of living and employers hike prices.

At the end of President Carter's term in office, the Council of Economic Advisers suggested a tax-based incomes policy (TIP).[17] The proposal provided that employees whose average pay increase was below an established standard would receive a tax credit. Alternatively, employees whose wage boosts exceeded the standard would be assessed a tax penalty. Conceptually, a tax-based policy would tend to overcome the distortion problem. By placing a ceiling only on the average rate of pay increase, firms could vary the relative pay of subgroups by means of merit pay and promotions and thereby encourage productivity. In theory, tax relief would also tend to preserve real wages, thereby alleviating the clamor for catch-up when the policy is relaxed.

Although a tax-based incomes policy represents a new and perhaps even desirable departure in combating inflation, it also suffers from a number of serious flaws that are likely to undermine its effectiveness. Of prime consideration is the administrative burden that would be created by its compliance requirements. Although the development of high-speed computers has made administration easier, a sizable bureaucracy was still required to manage the Carter administration's voluntary (and relatively ineffective) program. A tax-based policy would be even more cumbersome. To be equitable, it would have to require all firms to submit detailed records, unlike the voluntary program, where only large companies, the wage-price leaders, had to comply.

Although raising the specter of a "huge bureaucracy" is an appealing argument against a tax-based incomes policy, the administrative burden, though heavy, is not the only stumbling block to such a policy's successful implementation. The real problem is that an effective incomes policy that necessarily entails government intrusion into private decisionmaking goes strongly against the grain of the American ethos and hence lacks widespread support. This feeling has been sharpened by the inability of government to develop a tripartite

91

approach to policymaking which would call for a responsible role by business and labor in formulating and implementing anti-inflation policy. In turn, the lack of widespread support has led government to settle for temporary policies, thereby ensuring that pent-up pressures would reemerge once a stopgap program ended.

Incomes policies also bring into sharp focus the adversarial tenor of American industrial relations. U.S. labor leaders have viewed wage restraints as a threat to their right to bargain on behalf of their members. Moreover, both the business community and organized labor have argued that the rules of the game work against their constituencies. Business, for example, argued that the Nixon administration's wage-and-price-control policy crimped profit margins and curtailed investment funds, while labor claimed that wage earners had been short-changed because prices climbed far faster than earnings. Similar sentiments were voiced during the Carter administration's voluntary program, particularly because the major contributors to inflation during the period—energy, food, and interest charges—were largely outside the scope of the wage-price standards. Lacking business and labor support, the government was forced to act as sole arbitrator, and the parties involved were free to condemn the government for meddling.

Recognizing the difficulties of establishing an effective incomes policy, U.S. analysts have sought to glean lessons from the experience of industrial nations that have been relatively successful in combating inflationary pressures without resorting to excessive unemployment. In West Germany and Japan, wage bargaining takes place on an annual basis, while in the United States most contracts normally run for two or three years. Annual bargaining has two implications. First, contracts do not have to be indexed to take account of the rise in the cost of living; unanticipated price increases can be folded into the next year's contract. Second, annual negotiations tend to focus on the current state of the economy and industry or firm, thereby encouraging restraint during difficult economic periods. West German trade unions settled for moderate pay raises following the oil shocks of 1973 and 1979 because they were convinced that larger increases would reduce the ability of West German exporters to compete in foreign markets and thus would raise domestic unemployment. Similarly, in Japan, Ministry of Labor surveys found that wage settlements reflected company profit performance and product market conditions.

In the United States, pay increases pegged to cost-of-living increases have become almost universally accepted in principle. Recent concessions in industries facing dire circumstances are the exception and represented a temporary reaction to adversity, not a rejection of the principle. And even though only about 20 percent of the work force bargains collectively (compared with higher proportions in West Germany and Japan), union negotiations influence pay levels across the economy.

Escalator clauses tend to build past inflation into current wages and to reduce the effectiveness of monetary and fiscal policies in combating inflation. For example, if wages are fully indexed, one year's 7 percent inflation rate will lead to next year's 7 percent wage hike, thereby driving up next year's prices, and so forth. Moreover, indexing is not limited to pay alone. Pensions paid out under social security, as well as food stamps and other welfare payments, are pegged to the cost-of-living index. In an economy in which prices are rising, indexing can perpetuate or even accelerate inflationary trends.

Multiyear contracts obviously generate pressures for indexing. In an inflation-prone economy, union members are likely to reject agreements that fail to protect their standards of living, and labor negotiators who fail to protect their members' real earnings are soon out of a job. Bargainers are generally much more concerned with future price expectations than with company performance or conditions in the economy as a whole. Advocates of yearly bargaining assert that this timetable would make it easier for U.S. union representatives to offer temporary concessions, as their West German and Japanese counterparts have done. However, the claimed benefits of the annual bargaining in Japan and West Germany are contradicted by the experience of the United Kingdom, where, despite annual wage bargaining, pay increases have made a significant contribution

The United States is facing a period of both rapid adjustment and high unemployment, which makes transition more difficult and costly. Suggested solutions to ease the problems have ranged from trade protection measures that would slow down structural change, to requirements that products made abroad contain a specified percentage of inputs made in this country, to direct federal assistance to declining industries and labor surplus areas. This defensive response is understandable. At best, the benefits of improved productivity appear to be distant to affected workers, firms, and communities, requiring individual sacrifices of jobs, income, and community well-being. It is not surprising that the reaction of those affected is to preserve and protect their properties and jobs.

The difficulty with protective approaches is that rather than slowing down structural change, they often perpetuate inefficiencies and impair productivity and may be self-defeating in the long run. For example, if trade protection for one industry results in retaliation abroad, those industries which are producing competitively may be adversely affected and job losses may result.

In special cases, federal help for failing corporations may be prudent to salvage jobs and prevent massive dislocation of workers, particularly if the aid carries a quid pro quo involving productivity improvements. The bail out of the Chrysler Corporation offers an instructive lesson. It encouraged domestic competition and saved thousands of jobs. However, these protective approaches should be used with caution and on a case-by-case basis.

Because the interests of individual workers, firms, and communities do not necessarily coincide with the common good, at least in the short run, active policy intervention is justified to help the work force adjust to changing economic conditions. As John Stuart Mill said, ''There cannot be a more legitimate object of the legislator's care than the interests of those . . . who are sacrificed to the gains of their fellow citizens.''[1] A program of employment-adjustment assistance for workers displaced by structural change is one possible approach to the problem.

Employment-Adjustment Assistance

To date, public policy efforts to assist workers displaced from their jobs because of structural change have been haphazard. The programs established under the Manpower Development and Training Act (MDTA) in the 1960s were originally intended to respond to the problems of structural change. When it was found that those workers who were to be served had been reabsorbed into new jobs in a then-expanding economy, these training programs were refocused to deal with unskilled and deficiently educated workers. Another effort was mounted with the Trade Adjustment Act of 1962 and subsequent amendments, which provided limited funds for the retraining of workers who had lost their jobs because of imports. The training components of the law were rarely used, however, and the income support was criticized as being too generous. The Job Training Partnership Act of 1982 also offers retraining funds for displaced workers, but under current funding levels it can assist only a fraction of those who need retraining.

Unemployment compensation benefits provide temporary income support to the unemployed and are supplemented through collective-bargaining agreements in steel, autos, and a few other industries. However, for those who have lost their jobs permanently because of plant shutdowns, the regular unemployment insurance payments—twenty-six weeks in most states—are often too short to allow the displaced worker to find a new job. This is particularly true in periods of high unemployment or in areas hard hit by plant closures. In most states, workers lose their entitlement to unemployment benefits if they undertake training, for they are perceived as not being available for work while they are undergoing training. Administrative rules may also present obstacles to job search. Although workers can file claims for benefits in a state other than where they last worked, the procedure is slow and tends to inhibit mobility.

Existing training and unemployment insurance programs are inadequate instruments to provide for displaced workers. Under a more

97

comprehensive program, workers who were laid off because of trade or technological changes might be entitled to income maintenance, training allowances, and mobility grants. In addition to basic income support, laid-off workers could require training allowances to compensate for direct training costs. To assist workers who cannot find work in their own area, a mobility allowance could be used selectively to finance moving costs. A better labor-market information system also is needed to help workers who wish to relocate. Ironically, in an age of improved information technology, Michigan's laid-off auto workers relied on dated newsstand copies of Texas papers for information on job opportunities. While a national job bank may be impractical, regional listings of job vacancies by employers could be implemented. Simply putting classified advertisements from several regional newspapers into a computer would be a step forward. Providing information on local real estate markets might also help workers who are considering relocation. A transferring executive can now access that information through companies dealing in high-priced homes. This service could be extended to earners of more-moderate incomes, particularly if prices for communication of graphic and printed information made such information available at modest costs.

The alternative to relocating workers is to encourage new or expanding businesses to locate in labor surplus areas. The loss of industrial enterprises brings with it a loss of the tax base needed to support the social and physical infrastructure of a community. If this is not checked, it leads to waste of otherwise useful social capital—for schools, roads, sewer systems—which must be re-created elsewhere.

A regional policy that provides tax incentives or subsidized loans for new businesses to locate in depressed areas is one limited way to help these communities. While conceptually appealing, the U.S. experience with aid to depressed areas does not leave much room for optimism. As noted earlier, the tendency has been to spread the limited resources thinly. Economic developers have not succeeded in satisfying the multitudes with a few crumbs. In the small number of cases where government incentives succeeded in attracting new ventures to depressed areas, the firms, tending to be labor intensive, paid low wages, which was not a productivity-enhancing strategy. High-wage firms are likely to be attracted to a region for reasons other than tax incentives, such as modernized infrastructure, a skilled work force, or an attractive physical environment. It is not a coincidence that many new computer companies have been established around university towns in the Boston area or that Silicon Valley is close to centers of higher education and to the physical and cultural amenities offered by the Bay Area of California.

Clearly, the so-called smokestack communities cannot transform themselves into areas of natural beauty or establish centers of learning overnight. They can, however, seek to rebuild the physical infrastructure and work-force skills on which industries depend. As the income base of a community shrinks, its buildings, roads, and other infrastructure often fall into a state of disrepair. Another problem faced by declining areas is that the best and the brightest are the first to leave, thereby eroding the skill base of the community. Consequently, it appears that funding of selected regional public works projects and education and training programs could aid communities in maintaining their invested social capital while at the same time providing a source of skilled jobs for those willing to undertake training.

A program for employment adjustment could also include requirements of advance notification of mass layoffs or plant shutdowns. Most European countries require employers to give at least three months' notice before they make significant cutbacks in the size of the work force. In West Germany, six months' notice must be given if more than 10 percent of a company's work force is affected. With prenotification requirements, it would be possible to identify and provide preliminary job-search assistance to U.S. workers. At the same time, workers could be informed of various other adjustment-assistance programs, such as job retraining, for which they would become eligible.

A broad effort aimed at enhancing productivity performance cannot succeed without significant public outlays, but the benefits are likely to exceed the costs. In the absence of constructive government intervention to assist the victims of technological advances and free-trade policies, there is a danger that the goal of improving productivity and growth will be thwarted by self-defeating policies such as protectionism or special programs of assistance to groups with political clout.

Adapting the Work Force to Change

In addition to assisting those who are displaced by a changing economic structure, productivity is also likely to be improved if policies are aimed at increasing the adaptability of the work force. Greater job security is a prime ingredient in making change more palatable. Workers cannot be expected to exert extra efforts to raise their productivity if, by doing so, they put their jobs on the line. Education and training policies also have an important role to play in refocusing investments on productivity-enhancing activities which would ensure that an appropriately skilled labor force was there to meet the economy's needs.

Employment Security. The United States is unique among most other industrialized countries in tolerating unhindered layoffs during slack periods. West German legislation requires advance notification of layoffs and consultation between employers and workers' representatives to develop plans for retraining and re-employment. It also requires a lump-sum cash compensation for those dismissed. To deal with a short-term slack in demand, work-sharing is encouraged. Under this plan a firm may apply for funds from the unemployment insurance system to pay workers a proportion of the wages they lose by working less than full time.[2]

In Sweden, temporary subsidies have been given to companies that produced inventory stockpiles in order to keep a full work force on the job. Also, companies are encouraged to set aside part of their profits in earmarked tax-exempt investment reserves during periods of strong demand. During a downturn in activity, companies can withdraw these funds to invest in new plants or equipment.[3] Japanese companies resort to layoffs of temporary workers when demand falls, but they tend to retain their regular work force by assigning workers to other activities, including, on occasion, make-work projects such as cleaning the company's grounds.

In this country job-security measures are entirely a matter of individual company policy and concessions won by unions. A national policy could encourage the retention of employees during recessions by changing the regulations governing the unemployment insurance system. In the first place, companies could be dissuaded from laying off workers if they were required to make severance payments to dismissed employees or to carry the financial responsibility for extended unemployment benefits. In the second place, in most states, persons working a reduced number of hours per week generally have their unemployment benefits reduced by a dollar for each dollar earned, which tends to encourage layoffs rather than retention of workers on reduced schedules. California, however, has been experimenting with work-sharing for several years. For example, instead of laying off 20 percent of the work force, workers and employers participating in work-sharing programs agree to a 20 percent reduction in hours for all workers. The workers then receive a prorated share of the unemployment benefits to compensate for their lost earnings. California officials consider the program a success. Companies using work-sharing saved an average of $16 per worker each week in the taxes they contributed to the unemployment insurance fund compared with what they would have paid if employees had been laid off.[4]

Work-sharing might have a number of economic benefits, and experimentation by states should be encouraged. Continuing job attachment would keep workers' employment skills up-to-date. It could produce smaller swings in consumer spending since people working fewer hours would probably make smaller cutbacks in spending than unemployed workers. It might also reduce government outlays for social welfare programs. The work-sharing program

101

would be particularly beneficial to women and minorities because they generally tend to have the least seniority and are the first to go when layoffs occur.[5]

Training and Retraining. Recent government support for training has focused primarily on providing basic skills for the poorly educated, the unskilled, and the unemployed. For most of the U.S. work force, the acquisition and upgrading of skills is provided by employers, usually through on-the-job training. While this arrangement has a number of advantages, including cost effectiveness, there are a number of limitations. Given the accelerating pace of technological change, greater government support for employer training and retraining may prove necessary.

A key problem with current arrangements is cyclical vulnerability: training programs are the first to go in hard times. There is also little evidence of widespread adoption of retraining programs. Although most large companies with 10,000 or more employees provide some retraining for management or supervisory white-collar personnel, programs for manual workers are much rarer. Yet the latter will increasingly be required to adjust to a changing workplace. Moreover, while on-the-job training enables employees to perform specific tasks, a broader knowledge of why the tasks are performed and how they contribute to the production process as a whole may improve the way in which a worker does his or her job. Understanding these causal relationships may also enable workers to adapt to a greater range of job situations, which is particularly important considering the increasing applications of new technologies. While it is evident that employers, not the schools, are best equipped to provide the instruction, this type of training is expensive.

Incentives to develop broad-based training programs for employees could be provided most effectively through tax credits to employers. For instance, a firm introducing new technology that allows on-the-job training on the new equipment could qualify for a tax break. Such a program would be a logical complement to public policies aimed at increasing job security. If penalties are attached to layoffs, it is only fair to provide resources to enable companies to retrain their workers for productive activities.

Improving Basic Schooling. A nation's educational system affects the growth of its productivity. The educational attainment of the American labor force has risen rapidly since World War II as measured by the number of years spent in school. However, the competency of students in mastering the three R's has been falling for at least the past ten years, and it has been found to be well below the standards attained by other industrial nations. While the alarms may be exaggerated, there is room for genuine concern about the poor, if not negative, returns on the nation's investment in ever-longer education.

One key corrective action would be the establishment of national educational standards. America's fifty states and 17,000 school districts have jealously guarded their independence. Tradition has defended local school autonomy and rejected the notion of objective national competency tests. The only broadly accepted measure of achievement has been the length of time spent in school, but solid evidence indicates that number of years of schooling is too frequently a poor proxy for educational achievement. Neither the products of deficient schooling nor the labor market are well served when employers encounter high-school graduates who lack basic reading or computation skills. Without infringing on local autonomy, objective national standards could encourage the schools to concentrate resources on basic competency in reading, writing, and mathematics and would serve as a screening device for employers in selecting new workers.

It may also be appropriate to make some changes in established norms in the teaching profession. Uniform pay scales for teachers which ignore local labor market conditions need to be reevaluated. Schools—and their students—may suffer from the fact that a physics teacher receives the same pay as a physical education instructor. The labor market that places a high value on the skills of the physics teacher will outbid the schools for such teachers. If school system salary structures were to be more reflective of labor market realities, present shortages of such teachers could be alleviated. On the theory that what's good for the goose is also good for the gander, competency tests could be applied to the teachers as well as to pupils. In turn, teacher training would have to be reoriented from its present emphasis on methodology toward mastery of basic subject matter.

By continuing to tolerate a pool of unskilled and deficiently educated school leavers and marginally effective teachers, America forgoes the productive potential of a significant number of its citizens. The claim has already been advanced that the decline in the growth of U.S. productivity may be partially due to deficiencies in the nation's school systems. Most disadvantaged young people can be helped, through an increase in preschool and follow-through programs such as Head Start, compensatory education, remedial education, and self-paced computer-assisted instruction. These programs, together with basic adult education activities, could be made even more effective if they were geared to basic competency standards in secondary schools.[6]

Equity and Productivity

Other factors affect U.S. productivity in subtle but far-reaching ways. One is the distribution of the benefits of growth. Policies that clearly favor some while leaving others behind are likely to have an adverse effect on the economy in years to come. Whereas in 1960 the ''other'' America of poverty and deprivation was largely silent and unpoliticized, today those who perceive that they are unfairly treated are more likely to take action. One way to promote a more equitable sharing of economic benefits is for government to ensure that opportunities exist for those who want them.

In addition, a strong safety net must be in place for future and present members of society. Income maintenance is claimed by some to be a drag on the productive capacity of the economy, but how else can would-be workers support themselves while undergoing training if they have no other source of income? Similarly, many health and welfare activities have no direct, measurable relationship to productivity, yet they play an important role. Ill-fed children may suffer damage that permanently affects their ability to be educated and trained for productive work. The interaction of education, health, income, and jobs is nowhere more evident than in the well-known deplorable cycle that makes it difficult for many of the poor to improve their position.

The strength and productivity of the U.S. economy will be endangered if society continues to avoid facing the challenges of change. The ordeal of change, to borrow Eric Hoffer's apt phrase, should not fall on individuals who can least afford it. Progress cannot be accomplished without an active government role, a sense of social responsibility, and recognition of the links between efficiency and equity.

Actions by Business

Government policies can exert a positive influence on productivity, but ultimately, sustained progress depends upon the actions taken by companies, where the daily decisions made by managers and their employees have a direct and immediate impact on productivity. Management is well aware of the productivity problem and recognizes the need to concentrate company efforts on efficient production.

Sharing the Gains

Improved relations between labor and management are one means of boosting productivity. Although it is unrealistic to assume that labor and management would transform fundamentally long-established adversarial relations to focus on cooperation, steps can be taken within the traditional context to move them in more-productive directions. Two approaches seem most promising: greater job security and productivity bargaining. The two strategies are closely related.

Influenced by high unemployment, greater job security is already high on employee agendas, and it is likely to remain so in coming years as the work force ages, becoming more security conscious, and as changing technology continues to generate economic uncertainty. In contrast, employers are most interested in obtaining maximum flexibility in company operations and are therefore reluctant to guarantee job security and thereby incur additional costs. In fact, only about 10 percent of the work force covered by major bargaining agreements is protected by even such provisions as advance notification of shutdown.[7] The key to reconciling these different objectives lies in modifying work rules that prevent a flexible and efficient deployment of resources, and in developing job security and retraining policies that protect people rather than preserve jobs. The stimulus to this approach is that both workers and management will share in the improved productivity.

Job Security. In search for means to improve the efficiency of their operations, some companies have experimented with guaranteeing their workers greater employment security. Employees are more likely to accept changes in the organization of their work and to adapt to the advantages of new technologies if they do not fear that the net result of their efforts will be job or status loss. They are also more likely to develop a vested interest in the fortunes of the company and a greater identification with its goals. The key ingredient of such a policy is making it mutually advantageous to both management and employees. Management gains flexibility in decisionmaking, while employees' uncertainty about the ultimate results of those decisions is reduced.

The elements of an employment security program could include work-sharing rather than layoffs as a short-term response to difficulties, and reductions in the work force by attrition rather than by firings. Reductions by attrition could perhaps be supplemented by attractive early retirement provisions. In some cases the program could guarantee lifetime employment. These features could be accompanied by the provision of training to update skills when new techniques are introduced and by active policies of redeployment elsewhere within company operations with appropriate relocation allowances if a physical move is required. As Adam Smith noted, people are the hardest "baggage" to move. Unless they provide mechanisms by which to increase employee mobility, there is a danger that employment security programs will protect jobs and inefficient ways of doing work.

Productivity Bargaining. Most collective-bargaining agreements are concerned with routine issues of pay, work rules, overtime, and other bread-and-butter concerns. These agreements are sometimes hundreds of pages long and specify in detail working conditions, rules and regulations, labor rights, and management prerogatives.[8] In some contracts, constraints on management's flexibility to make temporary assignments of employees is spelled out in minute detail. Other rules limit the amount of work an employee may be called on to perform or may prevent an employee from being assigned to incidental work outside his or her strict classification. These rules were established to give workers day-to-day safeguards against arbitrary and capricious actions by management. However, as technology, materials, and production processes have changed, the rules have tended to inhibit productivity and to encourage management and labor to assert their rights according to the rule book rather than try to work cooperatively.

Productivity bargaining, in contrast, is a more collaborative effort, normally involving changes in basic work rules and trading greater job security for anticipated increases in productivity. The Fawley agreement reached between Esso Petroleum (U.K.) and its refinery workers in 1960 is an early example of productivity bargaining.[9] Faced with overmanning, low productivity, outdated equipment, and restrictive work practices, the company initiated, and the union agreed to, the formation of joint labor-management committees. With the guidance of an impartial consultant, the committees identified key production problems and developed the means to resolve them by negotiating mutually acceptable trade-offs between changes in work rules and changes in benefits. The trade-offs were acceptable to the workers because of "an assurance that there would be no dismissals, that basic wages would increase (providing greater security of in-

107

come), and that time spent at the refinery would be reduced."[10] In turn, the company was able to introduce modern technology and to reorganize work processes, thereby substantially increasing its productivity.

In the United States, longshoring, steel, and typesetting pioneered with productivity bargaining. Like the Fawley agreement, technological innovations stimulated greater cooperation between labor and management through collective bargaining. In longshoring, the use of containers in shipping required fundamental changes in work rules. These changes were accepted by the union in return for guarantees of job security for the regular work force and large, lump-sum payments for those who agreed to retire early. New typesetting technology brought similar arrangements in that industry, where, in return for the acceptance of automation, flexibility in job assignment, and new manning levels, the union won assurances of lifetime employment guarantees.

Less-publicized productivity bargaining has emerged recently as companies in financial difficulty have sought work-rule changes that increase productivity while offering workers greater employment security.[11] For example, several airline companies succeeded in negotiating significant changes in work rules covering their pilots' flying time and layovers by agreeing that no layoffs would result from the changes. In this case, the pilots accepted a loss of income under the new regulations because they were apparently convinced that their jobs depended on the companies' financial health. In other industries hard hit by the recession and increased competition, there are also signs of relaxing work rules in return for greater job or income security.

Productivity bargaining is a collaborative process. It involves joint problem-solving and acceptance of trade-offs, which places both labor and management outside their traditional roles. For management, productivity bargaining implies surrender of prerogatives by recognizing that the cooperation of labor is required to correct production deficiencies. For labor, productivity bargaining involves giving up hard-won work rules in exchange for a share of the gains from change. An essential element in productivity bargaining is the persuasion of labor and management that both stand to gain from successful negotiations.

Productivity Bonuses. Employees have an incentive to improve their performance if they stand to gain directly from their efforts.[12] Consequently another productivity-enhancing strategy is the development of a bonus system. The best-known plan was devised by Joseph Scanlon, a local steel union president, in the late 1930s. Under this system, workers are awarded cash bonuses based on the performance of the enterprise. In turn, they are encouraged to generate new ideas for improving productivity. Suggestions are taken up by production committees composed of elected workers and managers. Because one of the main objectives is to encourage teamwork and joint labor-management problem-solving to improve productivity, the bonus is based on the profits of the company as a whole rather than on the productivity of particular departments or production lines, and it is distributed to all employees, including management, supervisors, and support staff. Case studies indicate that a majority of the companies that have adopted Scanlon plans have experienced favorable results. Productivity improvements have been realized along with such intangibles as greater cooperation within the company, higher motivation, and greater acceptance of change.[13]

Despite the attractive features of Scanlon-type plans, only about 400 U.S. companies have adopted them. Far more prevalent in many American industries are piece-work incentive schemes that link earnings with the amount a worker actually produces. In theory this should encourage greater effort, but in practice the outcome may be the reverse when minimum targets become de facto maximums. Because these schemes tend to encourage competition among workers, they threaten the established status hierarchy within the group since older workers may be unable to match the pace of younger employees. There is consequently pressure to establish group norms to minimize competition. The schemes create a climate of continual conflict between labor and management over the piece rate set for the job, which may very well undermine productivity rather than increase it.

Employment-security productivity bargaining systems provide the means of attaining greater labor-management cooperation. While they do not represent a fundamental departure from adversarial positions, they tend to bring into sharper focus the shared objective of labor and management: to obtain a greater return for their efforts. The recognition of mutual interests may provide a firmer ground than exists at present for the establishment of programs to improve the quality of working life and increase workers' participation in company decisionmaking.

7

A More Productive Society

Ever since Adam Smith, economists have recognized the role that productivity growth plays in advancing economic prosperity and improving living standards. However, as long as the productivity process generated significant gains, most policymakers and citizens paid little attention to what was considered an esoteric subject.

For nearly three decades following World War II, most Americans found themselves better off each year, and they accepted the results as a natural development. Between 1948 and 1965 labor productivity in the business sector climbed at an annual rate of 3.2 percent. If sustained, this meant average real income would double in twenty-two years and multiply eightfold within the lifetime of the "baby boom" generation. Personal plans and public policy were influenced by these bright prospects as a highly productive nation moved forward to build a great society.

The optimism dissipated as serious problems appeared on the economic scene. Measured labor productivity dropped to an annual growth rate of 2.3 percent between 1965 and 1973—and below 1 percent in the following decade. Newer multifactor productivity estimates indicated similar declines, while foreign competitors were catching up and even surpassing American producers in key industries. These trends strongly influenced public and private attitudes. Many workers feared the loss of their jobs as foreign products outsold those made domestically, and individuals holding onto gainful employment were no longer confident that their children would enjoy as high a standard of living as they had. Those with the lowest incomes found that austerity can quickly alter the capacity and willingness of the more fortunate to share their blessings.

Today, public anxiety reflects the confusion surrounding the causes and cures of the decline in U.S. productivity growth. The quick and simple solutions offered by supply-side policies have failed to raise either investment or savings, and the resulting growth of the federal deficit threatens future growth. Similarly, analysts who place faith in the adoption of our chief competitors' policies to help reverse the lackluster productivity experience of the United States seem to have underestimated the difficulties of transplanting foreign experience. Our institutional setting is not necessarily a hospitable environment in which to nurture foreign practices. The confusion over defining industrial policies, as well as the ephemeral nature of many work-reform experiments, attests to this.

The decline in the growth of American productivity was avoidable, and a number of positive steps can now be taken to reverse the trend. Appropriate government policies are crucial to achieving this goal. Fighting inflation with a tight monetary policy has produced an unstable environment of high interest rates and high unemployment, which in turn have accounted for much of the productivity slowdown; thus the welcome relief from rising prices may be only temporary. Poor business conditions cut into productivity growth by hampering the ability of firms to make optimal use of their resources and by discouraging firms from investing in new plants and equipment, research and development, and the skills of their employees. Uncertainty about the future direction of policy acted as a further deterrent. The challenge is to develop a more effective and less costly antiinflationary strategy to attain sustained growth. One lesson emerges clearly from recent experience. To fight inflation with unemployment is to sacrifice productivity growth and ignore equity considerations.

Sustained progress on the productivity front requires institutional adjustments. Productivity growth requires easing, if not removing, obstacles to change. Past shifts from marginal farming and retailing to more productive opportunities in manufacturing and supermarkets were accomplished with little friction. Today the picture is different. High levels of unemployment, skill and geographical mismatches, the accelerating use of labor-saving technology, and the greater pressure of foreign competition have made adjustments more difficult and costly. Workers and their communities have understandably called for protection, and the government has the responsibility to help those facing displacement, not by erecting tariff barriers, but by instituting labor market policies that alleviate the burdens of adjustment. Advance notification concerning plant shutdowns, job-search assistance, income support, training, and subsidized mobility are key elements of public adjustment-assistance. If consensus could be reached, infrastructure investments targeted to hard-pressed communities could help declining areas maintain their social capital while at the same time providing a skilled work force for new or expanding firms choosing to locate in these areas.

Productivity is also likely to improve if public policies are aimed at increasing the adaptability of the work force. Greater job security is a crucial ingredient in the acceptance of change. Changing the regulations governing the unemployment system—e.g., making work-sharing a more widespread option—would help companies to stabilize employment. Education and training policies also have an important role to play.

The widely acknowledged deterioration of the public education system could be reversed by setting national performance standards for high-school pupils. Such standards would encourage the schools to concentrate on basic competency in the three R's and on imparting related knowledge that would ease the transfer from school to work. Changes that would make the norms of teacher pay and training more responsive to labor market realities would help schools attain and maintain these standards.

While many companies expend considerable resources on training,

113

little effort is focused on manual or clerical workers, who will bear the brunt of technological change in the immediate future. To encourage the ready adoption of new and efficient technologies, employers might be given targeted incentives—perhaps through tax credits—to make investments in the training and retraining of their work force. This strategy is also a logical complement to greater job security, for it encourages the protection of employees, not the preservation of outmoded jobs.

Government intervention will be necessary to achieve the twin goals of a more productive and more compassionate society. The value of the former will be diminished if it is not infused with a strong sense of equity. This means that the federal government must play an active and affirmative role in funding basic research and development, investing in social capital (physical as well as human), and helping the market (which is less than perfect) in the allocation process.

It is fashionable these days to blame the government for our problems. Indeed, the critics are on the mark in faulting the government for failing to discharge its responsibilities in achieving a more productive society, a society that would serve the common welfare.

Notes

1. The State of Productivity

1. Rudy Oswald, "Unions and Productivity," in *Productivity: Prospects for Growth,* ed. Jerome M. Rostow (New York: Van Nostrand Reinhold Co., 1981), p. 97.

2. Arnold Packer, "Productivity and Structural Change," *Strengthening the Economy: Studies in Productivity* (Washington, D.C.: Center for Democratic Policy, 1981).

3. U.S. Department of Labor, Bureau of Labor Statistics, *Comparative Growth in Manufacturing, Productivity, and Labor Costs in Selected Industrialized Countries,* Bulletin no. 1958 (Washington, D.C.: Department of Labor, 1977); and updated data from the Bureau of Labor Statistics.

4. Jerome A. Mark, "Productivity Measurement," in *Productivity: Prospects for Growth,* ed. Jerome M. Rostow (New York: Van Nostrand Reinhold Co., 1981), pp. 54–74.

5. Eli Ginsberg and George J. Vojta, "The Service Sector of the U.S. Economy," *Scientific American,* March 1981, p. 51.

6. National Research Council, Panel to Revive Productivity Statistics, *Measurement and Interpretation of Productivity* (Washington, D.C.: National Academy of Sciences, 1979), pp. 98 ff.

115

7. Ibid., pp. 125–26.

8. National Commission on Employment and Unemployment Statistics, *Counting the Labor Force* (Washington, D.C.: Government Printing Office, 1979), p. 163.

9. Sar A. Levitan, "The Work Ethic Lives," *Across the Board,* August 1979, p. 83.

10. Albert Rees, "Improving the Concepts and Techniques of Productivity Measure," *Monthly Labor Review,* September 1979, p. 27.

11. Paul S. Adler, "The Productivity Puzzle: Numbers Alone Won't Solve It," *Monthly Labor Review,* October 1982, p. 17.

2. The Productivity Problem: Macroeconomic Factors

1. John W. Kendrick, *Understanding Productivity* (Baltimore: Johns Hopkins University Press, 1977); and Solomon Fabricant, "The Productivity Issue: An Overview," in *Productivity: Prospects for Growth,* ed. Jerome M. Rostow (New York: Van Nostrand Reinhold Co., 1981), pp. 3–34.

2. Richard R. Nelson, "Research on Productivity Growth and Productivity Differences: Dead Ends and New Departures," *Journal of Economic Literature,* September 1981, pp. 1029–64.

3. Dale W. Jorgenson, "Accounting for Capital," in *Capital, Efficiency, and Growth,* ed. George M. von Furstenberg (Cambridge, Mass.: Ballinger, 1980); Otto Eckstein, "Core Inflation, Productivity, Capital Supply, and Demand Management," in *The Economy and the President: 1980 and Beyond,* ed. Walter E. Hoadley (Englewood Cliffs, N.J.: Prentice-Hall, 1980); Peter K. Clark, "Issues in the Analysis of Capital Formation and Productivity Growth," *Brookings Papers on Economic Activity,* no. 2, 1979 (Washington, D.C.: Brookings Institution, 1979), pp. 423–31; and Council of Economic Advisers, *Economic Report of the President* (Washington, D.C.: Government Printing Office, 1982), pp. 77 ff.

4. Edward F. Denison, *Accounting for Slower Economic Growth: The United States in the 1970s* (Washington, D.C.: Brookings Institution, 1979).

5. U.S. Department of Labor, Bureau of Labor Statistics, *News Release*, April 6, 1983.

6. J. R. Norsworthy and Michael Harper, "The Role of Capital Formation in the Recent Slowdown in Productivity Growth," Bureau of Labor Statistics Working Paper no. 87, January 1979.

7. Organisation for Economic Co-operation and Development, *Economic Outlook* (Paris, December 1981), p. 133.

8. Martin Neil Bailey, "Productivity and the Services of Capital and Labor," *Brookings Papers on Economic Activity,* no. 1, 1981 (Washington, D.C.: Brookings Institution, 1981), pp. 1–66; L. R. Christensen, D. Cummings, and D. Jorgensen, "Economic Growth, 1947–1973: An International Comparison," in *New Developments in Productivity Measurement and Analysis,* ed. John W. Kendrick and B. Vaccara (Chicago: University of Chicago Press, 1980); and John W. Kendrick, *Sources of Growth in Real Product and Productivity in Eight Countries, 1960–1978* (New York: New York Stock Exchange, 1980).

9. Council of Economic Advisers, *Economic Report of the President* (Washington, D.C.: Government Printing Office, 1979), p. 69.

10. U.S. Congress, Joint Economic Committee, *Monetary Policy, Selective Credit Policy, and Industrial Policy in France, Britain, West Germany, and Sweden* (Washington, D.C.: Government Printing Office, 1981), p. 120.

11. Gregory B. Christensen and Robert H. Haveman, "Running Out of Gas," *Executive,* Fall 1980, pp. 31–32; and E. A. Hudson and Dale Jorgenson, "Energy Prices and the U.S. Economy, 1972–1976," *Natural Resource Journal,* October 1978, pp. 877–97.

12. Ishag Nadim, "Sectoral Productivity Slowdown," *American Economic Review,* May 1980, pp. 349–52.

13. Council of Economic Advisers, *Economic Report of the President* (1979), p. 69.

14. Victor R. Fuchs, *Economic Growth and the Rise of Service Employment,* NBER Reprint no. 257 (Cambridge, Mass.: National Bureau of Economic Research, 1982), pp. 239–40.

15. Council of Economic Advisers, *Economic Report of the President* (1979), p. 70.

16. Organisation for Economic Co-operation and Development, *Economic Outlook* (Paris, July 1979), pp. 28–35.

17. Lester C. Thurow, *The Zero-Sum Society* (New York: Penguin Books, 1981), pp. 86–88.

18. Mary Jane Bolle, *Impact of the Business Cycle on Productivity Growth in the U.S. Economy* (Washington, D.C.: Congressional Research Service, 1982).

19. New York Stock Exchange, *U.S. Economic Performance in a Global Perspective* (New York, 1981).

20. Organisation for Economic Co-operation and Development, *Economic Surveys: Germany* (Paris, 1981).

21. Organisation for Economic Co-operation and Development, *Economic Surveys: Japan* (Paris, 1981).

3. The Productivity Problem: Institutional Factors

1. Joseph A. Schumpeter, *The Theory of Economic Development* (Cambridge, Mass.: Harvard University Press, 1949), pp. 58, 63.

2. John F. Tomer, "Worker Motivation: A Neglected Element in Micro-Micro Theory," *Journal of Economic Issues,* June 1981, pp. 351–62; Richard D. Rosenberg and Eliezer Rosenstein, "Participation and Productivity: An Empirical Study," *Industrial and Labor Relations Review,* April 1980, pp. 355–67; and Kenneth Walker, "Workers' Participation in Management," *International Institute for Labour Studies Bulletin,* no. 12, 1974.

3. Harvey Leibenstein, "A Branch of Economics is Missing: Micro-Micro Theory," *Journal of Economic Literature,* June 1979, pp. 477–502.

4. Johannes Schregle, "Codetermination in the Federal Republic of Germany: A Comparative View," *International Labour Review,* January–February 1978, pp. 81–90.

5. Benjamin C. Roberts et al., *Collective Bargaining and Em-*

ployee Participation in Western Europe, North America, and Japan (New York: Trilateral Commission, 1979), pp. 41 ff.

6. Organisation for Economic Co-operation and Development, *The Development of Industrial Relations Systems: Some Implications of Japanese Experience* (Paris, 1977).

7. Robert E. Cole, *Work, Mobility, and Participation* (Berkeley: University of California Press, 1979), p. 166.

8. Organisation for Economic Co-operation and Development, *Youth Without Work* (Paris, 1981), pp. 88–156.

9. Organisation for Economic Co-operation and Development, *The Development of Industrial Relations Systems,* p. 17.

10. Anthony P. .Carnevale and Harold Goldstein, *Employee Training: Its Changing Role and an Analysis of New Data* (Washington, D.C.: American Society for Training and Development, 1983), pp. 44–60.

11. Robert H. Hayes and William J. Abernathy, "Managing Our Way to Economic Decline," *Harvard Business Review,* July–August 1980. A contrary view is presented by Richard R. West and Dennis E. Logue in "The False Doctrine of Productivity," *New York Times,* January 9, 1983.

12. Committee for Economic Development, *Productivity Policy: Key to the Nation's Economic Future* (Washington, D.C., 1983), pp. 42 ff.

13. *Business Week,* May 11, 1981, p. 86.

14. Cole, *Work, Mobility, and Participation,* p. 166.

15. Steven Parnes, *Productivity and the Quality of Working Life* (Scarsdale, N.Y.: Work in America Institute, 1978), p. 4.

16. New York Stock Exchange, Office of Economic Research, *People and Productivity: A Challenge to Corporate America* (New York, 1982).

17. Sar A. Levitan and Clifford M. Johnson, *Second Thoughts on Work* (Kalamazoo, Mich.: W. E. Upjohn Institute for Employment Research, 1982), pp. 173–99.

18. Archie Kleingartner and Ross E. Azevedo, "Productivity

Bargaining and Organizational Behavior,'' in *Collective Bargaining and Productivity,* ed. Gerald Somers (Madison, Wis.: Industrial Relations Research Association, 1975), pp. 119–39.

19. Irving H. Siegel and Edgar Weinberg, *Labor-Management Cooperation: The American Experience* (Kalamazoo, Mich.: W. E. Upjohn Institute for Employment Research, 1982).

4. Prospects for the Next Decade

1. Juan Rada, *The Impact of Microelectronics* (Geneva: International Labour Office, 1980).

2. Robert Taggart, *A Fisherman's Guide: An Assessment of Training and Remediation Strategies* (Kalamazoo, Mich.: W. E. Upjohn Institute for Employment Research, 1981).

3. American Electronics Association, *Technical Employment Projections* (Palo Alto, Calif., 1981).

4. H. R. Bowen and Garth L. Mangum, eds., *Automation and Economic Progress: A Summary Report of the National Commission on Technology, Automation, and Economic Progress* (Englewood Cliffs, N.J.: Prentice-Hall, 1966), p. 10.

5. Ronald E. Kutscher, ''New Economic Protections Through 1990—An Overview,'' *Monthly Labor Review,* August 1981, pp. 9–17.

6. Diane Werneke, *Microelectronics and Office Jobs: The Impact of the Chip on Women's Employment* (Geneva: International Labour Office, 1983).

7. Levitan and Johnson, *Second Thoughts on Work,* p. 125.

8. Council of Economic Advisers, *Economic Report of the President* (Washington, D.C.: Government Printing Office, 1983), p. 58.

5. Less or More Government

1. Lee Bawden and Frank Levy, ''The Economic Well-Being of Families and Individuals,'' in *The Reagan Experiment,* ed. John L. Palmer and Isabel V. Sawhill (Washington, D.C.: Urban Institute Press, 1982), pp. 474–80.

2. Kenneth McLennan, "Strategy for Growth," *Executive*, Fall 1980, pp. 33–34.

3. Charles R. Hulten and June A. O'Neill, "Tax Policy," in *The Reagan Experiment*, p. 121.

4. Organisation for Economic Co-operation and Development, *Long Term Trends in Tax Revenues of OECD Member Countries, 1955–1980* (Paris, 1981).

5. Council of Economic Advisers, *Economic Report of the President* (Washington, D.C.: Government Printing Office, 1981), pp. 80–82.

6. Taggart, *A Fisherman's Guide*, pp. 280–94.

7. Marc Bendick, "Employment, Training, and Economic Development," in *The Reagan Experiment*, p. 254.

8. Committee for Economic Development, *Productivity Policy*, p. 41.

9. OECD, *Inventory of Adjustment Measures in the Industrial Sector Taken by Member Governments since 1974* (Paris, 1979), pp. 55–59; and *Economic Surveys: Japan.*

10. Joint Economic Committee, *Monetary Policy, Selective Credit Policy and Industrial Policy in France, Britain, West Germany, and Sweden*, p. 9.

11. Ibid., pp. 34–35.

12. Ibid., pp. 99–129.

13. Congressional Budget Office, *The Productivity Problem: Alternatives for Action* (Washington, D.C.: Government Printing Office, 1981), pp. 126–27.

14. Mancur Olson, *The Rise and Decline of Nations* (New Haven, Conn.: Yale University Press, 1982).

15. Ginsberg and Vojta, "The Service Sector of the U.S. Economy," p. 55.

16. Barry Bluestone and Bennett Harrison, *The Deindustrialization of America* (New York: Basic Books, 1982).

17. Council of Economic Advisers, *Economic Report of the President* (1981), p. 64.

6. Labor Market Policies

1. John Stuart Mill, *Principles of Political Economy,* ed. William J. Ashley (London: Longmans, Green and Co., 1926), p. 99.

2. Carol L. Jusenius and Burkhard von Rabeneu, "Unemployment Statistics: Problems of International Comparison," *Data Collection, Processing, and Presentation,* appendix vol. 2 of *Counting the Labor Force* (Washington, D.C.: Government Printing Office, 1979).

3. Diane Werneke, "Women's Employment in Recession and Recovery," *International Labour Review,* January–February 1979, pp. 45–48.

4. Judith Cummings, "Novel Ways Being Used to Save Jobs," *New York Times,* January 29, 1982, p. A10.

5. Sar A. Levitan, Garth Mangum, and Ray Marshall, *Human Resources and Labor Markets,* 3rd ed. (New York: Harper and Row, 1981), p. 55.

6. Taggart, *A Fisherman's Guide.*

7. Siegel and Weinberg, *Labor-Management Cooperation,* p. 163.

8. D. Quinn Mills, "Reforming the U.S. System of Collective Bargaining," *Monthly Labor Review,* March 1983, pp. 18–22.

9. Allen Flanders, *The Fawley Productivity Agreement* (London: Faber and Faber, 1964).

10. R. B. McKersie and L. C. Hunter, *Pay, Productivity, and Collective Bargaining* (London: Macmillan, 1973), p. 62.

11. Robert S. Greenberger, "Work Rule Changes Quietly Spread as Firms Try to Raise Productivity," *Wall Street Journal,* January 25, 1983, p. 35.

12. Committee for Economic Development, *Productivity Policy,* pp. 82–84.

13. Siegel and Weinberg, *Labor-Management Cooperation,* p. 186.

Index

About the Authors

Sar A. Levitan is Research Professor of Economics and Director of the Center for Social Policy Studies at the George Washington University. His previous books include *Working for the Sovereign: Employee Relations in the Federal Government* (with Alexandra B. Noden) and *Business Lobbies: The Public Good and the Bottom Line* (with Martha R. Cooper). **Diane Werneke** is a research economist on the staff of Senator Paul Tsongas. She is author of *Microelectronics and Office Jobs: The Impact of the Chip on Women's Employment Opportunities*.